More advance praise for
Solving the Corporate Value Enigma:

"A must-read for executives who strive to capture that 40 percent of potential shareholder value they know is sitting on the table, but never had a 'how-to' handbook for proceeding to close the gap."
—Peter J. DiConza, JD, President and CEO, DiConza Industries, Inc.

"Manganelli and Hagen solve the corporate enigma. A must-read in these perilous times."
—Elizabeth Ann (Betsy) Kovacs, President & CEO,
Association of Management Consulting Firms

"A new perspective on how to use the elements of an organization as a value system to drive profit, performance, and growth."
—Rick Radecki, Delphi Automotive Systems

"A blueprint to become a competitive 'sense-and-respond' organization; maximizing short-term return and long-term equity by closing 'the value gap.'"
—Maria Newport, President, Newport O'Connor
Executive Search and Consulting

"The really good managers have always known that the performance levels of their organizations fall far short of their potentials. *Solving the Corporate Value Enigma* lays out a proven and solid method for closing this gap."
—Richard Metzler, Trove Partners, LLC

"This book provides a concise outline that identifies the many variables to be conquered to unleash hidden value within corporations."
—Christopher J. Mahler, National Sales Manager, Weeden & Company

"By combining systems theory with decision analysis, Manganelli and Hagen have 'broken the code' with respect to unlocking shareholder value."
—Kevin Minds, Director, Mobile Broadband Solutions,
Boeing Homeland Security and Services

"Insightful and substantive. An eminently readable business book."
—Ford Harding, author of *Cross-Selling Success*

Solving the Corporate Value Enigma "combines clear, practical insights with a system for increasing the value organizations provide their shareholders."
—Dan Cabbell, Manager Six Sigma, Space Systems Division,
Electronic Systems Sector, Northrop Grumman

"A must-read for executives in every industry, including healthcare. It is the first book to so articulately link shareholder value to user-friendly practical tools that make a difference."

—Anne Marie Flynn, MA, RN, Principal, Results Consulting Practice

"*Solving the Corporate Value Enigma* . . . sets the bar high, avoiding the trap of most management books of the poorly aimed shotgun blast of supposed 'best practices.' Instead, it provides a systems approach to optimizing the one true core competency, the one that is the soul of a company; namely, how it makes decisions."

—Art Gemmer, Principal Risk Analyst, Rockwell Collins, Inc.

"Drs. Manganelli and Hagen's latest effort, *Solving the Corporate Value Enigma: A System to Unlock Shareholder Value,* should be mandatory reading for all who are engaged in the management of business organizations, from CEOs to business students."

—Thomas F. Keenan, Vice President and Chief Operating Officer, International Marine Corporation

"Can it be that up to 40 percent of potential shareholder value is being left on the table? Ray Manganelli and Brian Hagen not only show why, but how to recapture this value. An insightful read for any CEO."

—Steve Sashihara, President and CEO, Princeton Consultants, Inc.

"An excellent and practical guide for senior executives to transform their businesses by managing the four components of value—business strategy, asset portfolios, financial measures and structure, and organization and operations—as a system."

—Jill Totenberg, President and CEO, The Totenberg Group

"A radical and thought-provoking journey for executives willing to see beyond conventional myopia and into value-added business visions and results."

—John D. Thompson II, Founder & President, The Links Group LLC

"Each chapter provides unique insights and methods for achieving revenue growth. A must-read for all business leaders."

—Dr. Alexander R. Giaquinto, Vice President, Worldwide Regulatory Affairs, Schering-Plough Corporation

"*Solving the Corporate Value Enigma* breaks new ground in the value equation."

—John S. Bliss, Principal, Bliss, Gouverneur & Associates

"A great guide for value-based management principles . . . a must-read for all senior and mid-level executives."

—Andrew L. Lux, Ph.D., Vice President, Operations, Renal Division, Baxter Healthcare Corporation

Solving the
Corporate Value Enigma

Solving the
Corporate Value Enigma

A System to Unlock Shareholder Value

Raymond L. Manganelli
and Brian W. Hagen

AMACOM
American Management Association
New York • Atlanta • Brussels • Buenos Aires • Chicago • London • Mexico City
San Francisco • Shanghai • Tokyo • Toronto • Washington, D.C.

Special discounts on bulk quantities of AMACOM books are
available to corporations, professional associations, and other
organizations. For details, contact Special Sales Department,
AMACOM, a division of American Management Association,
1601 Broadway, New York, NY 10019.
Tel.: 212-903-8316. Fax: 212-903-8083.
Web site: www.amacombooks.org

This publication is designed to provide accurate and authoritative
information in regard to the subject matter covered. It is sold with the
understanding that the publisher is not engaged in rendering legal,
accounting, or other professional service. If legal advice or other
expert assistance is required, the services of a competent professional
person should be sought.

Library of Congress Cataloging-in-Publication Data

Manganelli, Raymond L.
    Solving the corporate value enigma : a system to unlock shareholder
value / Raymond L. Manganelli and Brian W. Hagen.
      p.   cm.
    Includes bibliographical references and index.
    ISBN 0-8144-0692-0
    1. Corporations—Valuation.   2. Corporations—Growth.   3.
Corporations—Accounting.   4. Strategic planning.   5. Corporate
profits.   I. Hagen, Brian W., 1957–   II. Title.
  HG4028.V3 M3254 2003
  658.15—dc21   2002014683

Printing number

10   9   8   7   6   5   4   3   2   1

To our families
Cathy, Tom, and Christopher Manganelli
and
Mine, Koray, and Altay Hagen,
who have encouraged, inspired,
and shared in all of our best work.

Contents

Chapter 5:
Organization and Operations   141

Chapter 6:
The Final Frontier   181

Preface

Scientists have long contended that the human organism uses only about 10 percent of its brain "power," mysteriously leaving some 90 percent untapped and unexplored. For several years now, we have considered that the corporate organism represents an analogous mystery, where much of its "power"—its value both identified and delivered—similarly goes untapped and unexplored. And while we will leave the human brain's mystery to others, we set out to solve the mystery of the corporate organism: the corporate value enigma.

As we write this preface late in 2002, we find business in perilous times:

- The Dow is down almost 40 percent in two years
- Real GDP in the United States is predicted to grow at the mediocre rate of some 2 percent
- The frequency of CEO turnover has doubled in five years
- More than 60 percent of mergers and acquisitions since 1995 have destroyed shareholder value
- Consumer confidence is approaching record lows

But twenty years of professional practice experience, combined with our recent extensive executive interview survey of 500 major corporations in ten industries, provides evidence that perilous times can provide major opportunities as well as the obvious challenges:

- Surveyed senior executives report significant opportunities for enhanced growth, improved performance, and increased profits in these turbulent markets.

■ Our experience provides extensive evidence that corporate investments made in the "turbulent trough" yield substantially greater rates-of-return than investments made at other points in the cycle.

■ Surveyed senior executives identify the same consistent set of "levers" to pull—in both good and bad markets—to optimize corporate value.

So the turbulent markets brought on by these perilous times can provide an even greater opportunity for investment and return by "unfreezing" traditional market structures and by catalyzing the rate of innovation and change.

This book is written for use in all business climates: the prosperous as well as the perilous. It is intended to serve as a resource for executives to unlock the shareholder value that they readily admit is currently held captive within their organizations. The book presents:

A Survey: the results from the most comprehensive set of executive interviews ever conducted focusing on a systematic approach to optimizing shareholder value.

A System: the comprehensive discussion of a "system of value," presenting the five essential rules for optimizing the alignment of the four interdependent system components: business strategy, asset portfolio, financial measures and structure, and organization and operations.

A Methodology: the step-by-step roadmap to achieve up to 40 percent more value from the corporation, including methods, tools, techniques, and tips.

A Thirty-Day "Turbo" Launch Program: the thirty-day accelerated program to implement the system and get to "quick win" results in the current quarter.

A Case: the extended "composite" case study that illustrates the deployment of the entire system in a real-life setting, as well as many other historical and current examples.

The book is intended for the variety of readers concerned with optimizing corporate shareholder value, including:

Senior Executives/General Management: to help them move their corporations onto the "efficient frontier," optimizing the relationship between short-term earnings and long-term value creation.

Functional Unit Heads: to help them understand the interdependence of the four sources of corporate value.

Business Improvement Practitioners: to help them learn a practical and quick methodology to optimize the value of the corporation.

Analysts: to help them assess corporate value potential and performance in a new and remarkable way.

Investors: to help them evaluate targeted firms for investment and for portfolio balance.

Trainers: to help them prepare training programs to apply the five rules of value optimization.

General Business Readers: to help them experience a comprehensive, quantitative, systematic approach to optimizing corporate value.

Enjoy the book!

Special Acknowledgments

The act of writing a book as coauthors is always a collaboration. In this specific case, the collaboration went well beyond the two of us: It was a collaboration with our colleagues at Strategic Decisions Group (SDG).

Special thanks go to those who founded SDG—Jeff Foran, Ron Howard, Jim Matheson, and Carl Spetzler—as they helped to develop the intellectual foundation on which this work is built. Special thanks also to our other colleagues at SDG who have expanded this intellectual property greatly. In particular, we thank Mike Allen, author of *Business Portfolio Management,* who conceived of the portfolio approach we describe in this book.

In addition, Robin Arnold and Jim Lang provided leadership, encouragement, and support for the development of this work at SDG, as did many others there.

We are grateful to SDG for granting us permission to use its intellectual property in our book.

Acknowledgments

We acknowledge with much gratitude those who helped make this book possible:

From Strategic Decisions Group: James Bonine, Michele Cinque, and Catherine Donelan.

From the American Management Association: Ray O'Connell and Ed Selig

And to all of our clients, colleagues, and comrades, who have the courage, the vision, and the perseverance to search for the solution to the corporate value enigma.

Corporate Value's Enigma

CHAPTER ONE

"We will, we will, rock you."

—THE ROCK GROUP QUEEN

This book will shock you. It will shock you reading it as it shocked us writing it. Because in explaining an enigma—the mystery of why senior executives knowingly sub-optimize the performance of their enterprises to the tune of 40 percent—we discovered a startling truth. And that truth will shock you.

From a Greek word for story, *enigma* has come to mean the mysterious, the baffling, and the inexplicable. It connotes not just a puzzle, but something of much larger significance—the deeply mystifying phenomenon, which, if only we could decode it, would teach us a great and useful truth.

Solving an enigma requires moving from a state of confusion and myopia to a state of enlightenment and vision. Solving an enigma requires clarity in both thought and action. Transparency is key as each step taken and conclusion drawn must logically fit in relation with other steps leading to the solution. Unsolved enigmas are subject to superstition, traditions, illogical thought, and wrongful action.

As you will come to understand over the next few pages, corporate value is an enigma from many perspectives. Corporate executives clearly understand that driving the corporation's stock price is a virtuous cycle of activities rewarding shareholders, employees, creditors, lenders, and community alike. But how to create and drive that virtuous cycle is clearly not well understood by the executives throughout the organization nor well communicated to the stock analysts that influence the corporation's stock performance. In the post-Enron/WorldCom/Tyco/Adelphia era, corporations will become stock performance leaders through the clarity and transparency of their thoughts, visions, decisions, actions, and reporting that ultimately drive their value creation. This book will both reveal the enigma of corporate value and detail how to achieve clarity and transparency in corporate value creation, thus helping to eliminate the hurdles to superior stock price performance and ensure significant, if not industry leading, shareholder value gains.

But first we must understand what the enigma of corporate value is. What are the underlying sources and systems of corporate value? When we set out to do the most detailed research ever done anywhere on the sources and systems of corporate value, we certainly had our expectations. But what we found surpassed our expectations in numerous ways, providing both enlightenment and then the vision for solving the enigma of corporate value.

Building on more than twenty years of professional practice experience in working with hundreds of companies and their senior executives, we conducted detailed interviews with about 500 senior executives—each from a different major company—spread across ten industries. In addition, more than 1,000 executives participated in Web-based surveys. While that research was going on, the American economy was hit with the unparalleled combination of three simultaneous business disruptions. First, after one of the longest periods of economic expansion in history, we plunged into a recession that came quickly and without warning. Second, the attacks on the World Trade Center and the Pentagon on September 11, 2001, sent shock waves through the country and deepened the recession. Third, the collapse of Enron resulted in the largest bankruptcy in American history. It was followed all too quickly by the collapse of WorldCom and other major corporations, and jangled the nerves of a market that wondered what other debacles might be lurking inside of other corporations with accounting structures. With one voice, the pundits told us that everything had changed, including business basics. But that's not what our research revealed.

Three hundred of our interviews took place in the second quarter of 2001. Then came the recession, 9/11, and the collapse of Enron. In the first quarter of 2002, we interviewed executives at an additional 200 companies. And in March of 2002, we polled another 300 executives, through our Web-based survey, about the specific recommendations offered here. What we found is that executives in 2002 responded to issues of strategy, assets, finance, and operations precisely as they had responded in 2001 and earlier.

Our comprehensive research over the two years ending in 2002 has validated the startling and sobering truth that best business practices haven't changed in more than twenty years of hands-on, in-depth professional practice across industries and continents. Our research revealed that:

- Senior executives know that they squander 40 percent of potential shareholder value.

    1. *Top Down* (looking at what is lost): Executives report creating only 60 percent of what is possible to create with their corporations.

2. *Bottom Up* (looking at what can be gained): Executives report, in a separate but amazingly correlated statistic, that they can add 40 percent more value by leading and managing the enterprise differently.

3. *Unidentified Value:* We have found that in the last twenty years that there has been from 30 percent to 100 percent more value available to senior executives than they are currently able to identify.

■ Senior executives know and agree that shareholder value is a system with four interdependent parts—business strategy, asset portfolios, financial measures and structure, and organization and operations—and that all the value comes from managing these four interdependent components together as a whole. Yet even with this knowledge, only a small number of executives ever attempt to manage their enterprises this way, and what's more, their estimate of the potential results of taking this action is that it would amazingly and completely transform the business.

To be blunt: Executives know how much value they are leaving on the table. They know what they must do to capture it. And they know how large the reward is for doing so. That broad agreement and the unchanging nature of business basics, no matter how great the economic shocks, would have been news enough.

But we found near unanimity in another area as well: More than two thirds of companies aren't even trying to do what it takes to capture that additional 40 percent in value. That is the *enigma of corporate value,* the contradiction that stuns even the most casual observer: *Despite knowing precisely what they must do and how enormous the rewards are for doing it, the overwhelming majority of companies don't even make the attempt.*

The 40 Percent Gap

Why a gap of 40 percent in value? In simple terms, corporate value capture can be thought of in two terms:

1. Value Potential Identified (VPI): The percentage of the "ultimate value" that the corporation's strategy identifies
2. Value Potential Delivered (VPD): The percentage of the strategy's value that the corporation delivers

Consequently, corporate value capture can be thought of as the following product of terms: Corporate Value Capture equals the Value Potential Identified times the Value Potential Delivered, or:

$$\% \text{ Corporate Value Capture} = \text{VPI} \times \text{VPD}$$

Senior executives report that their current strategy targets, on average, only about 75 percent of the potential value of their organization, or VPI = 75 percent (see Exhibit 1-1). They also report their organizations deliver, on average, only about 75 percent of the potential value of their strategies, or VPD = 75 percent (Exhibit 1-2). The value actually captured of that total potential value is illustrated in Exhibit 1-3, showing that the typical organization is capturing only about 60 percent of the value available to it. This leaves a "value gap" of 40 percent (see Exhibit 1-4).

By comparison, a 40 percent drop in sales, revenues, or stock price would command the urgent attention of the CEO and even the board. The 40 percent gap in value should raise the same red flags that a 40 percent shortfall in other measures would undoubtedly raise. Yet, it doesn't, since most companies are apparently content to live with that shortfall.

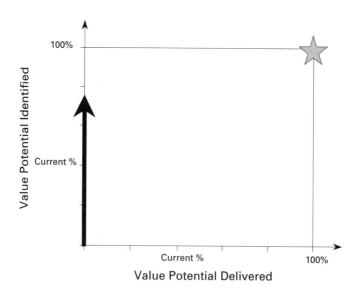

Exhibit 1-1 – Current strategy identifies only about 75 percent of the potential value of organizations.

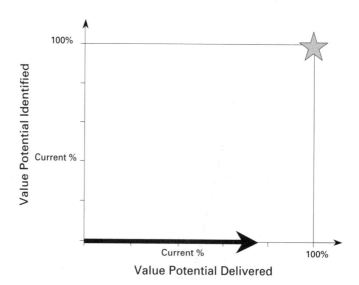

Exhibit 1-2 – Organizations deliver only about 75 percent of the potential value of their strategies.

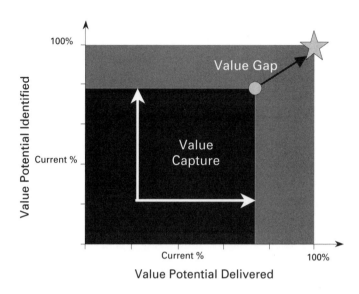

Exhibit 1-3 – Organizations capture only about 60 percent of their value potential.

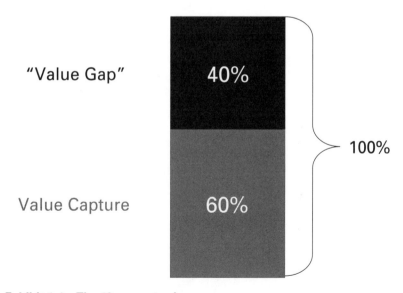

Exhibit 1-4 – The 40 percent value gap.

The enigma surrounds not only the failure to pursue optimal value, but also entails further enigmas about each of the value system's interdependent parts—strategy, assets, finance, and organization and operations—as illustrated by the results of our surveys:

- More than 70 percent of executives surveyed report that it is critical to understand the impact of risk on strategy; yet only a small minority identifies and measures risk. Why choose to ignore what you yourself have identified as the critical component of value?
- On average, executives surveyed report that at least 20 percent of all their companies' assets are worth more to some other company or organization than they are to their own organization; yet their companies neither attempt to increase the value of those assets to themselves nor try to sell them. Why not improve or liquidate the assets?
- Almost 95 percent of organizations surveyed report that they do *not* measure shareholder value using a single primary measure or an integrated set of measures. While they do *not* adequately measure shareholder value, they report that it is their primary responsibility to increase it. How can you improve what you do not measure?
- Sixty-eight percent of organizations surveyed report that their organizational structure impedes the implementation of their strategy, yet those same executives designed and now control these same organizational structures. Why not change them?

These findings defy logic. Why don't companies quantitatively measure risk when they know it is critical to strategy? Why do they sit on assets instead of improving or divesting them? Why do they tolerate an organization that impedes strategy? In short, why are most executives satisfied with such a small portion of the value they've identified when they could deliver so much additional value to all the stakeholders of the corporation, including themselves?

Consider financial measures. It is a truism, known to all executives, that what is measured gets done, that you can only improve what you measure, and that what gets measured is what absorbs most of the attention of the organization. Yet only 6 percent of the surveyed companies employ an integrated set of measures for shareholder value. The other 94 percent are willing to live a contradiction that may be discomfiting but apparently not as discomfiting as attempting to solve it. Why?

Because the "value gap" remains invisible and, until now, has gone largely unquantified; it registers with most executives only as a vague dissatisfaction or a nagging sense that the organization could do a lot better. But the unease runs even deeper, as we have discovered. Executives don't do what they know they must for one simple reason: they don't know how. Uncertainty about the *how* saps the *will* to make the attempt. Why attempt to get 40 percent breakthrough performance when no one is asking for it, when no one knows it's there? The very attempt becomes an act of self-exposure, of increased and burdensome expectations, of seemingly unnecessary and manufactured risk. The result: the enigma of corporate value.

That explains the enigma, but it doesn't solve it. Managing strategy, assets, financial measures, and organization and operations as a system has proven to be far more difficult than originally thought—as the brief shelf life of each successive management bromide has demonstrated. But if the business basics haven't changed, neither have the problems. From the time of Frederick W. Taylor forward, systems management has remained the central difficulty for executives.[1]

To achieve efficiency and productive power, complex endeavors are broken into ever smaller units, ever smaller tasks. The problem for senior executives is to put all the pieces back together again, then to put the resulting bigger pieces together, and finally, to put together the whole and operate it as one, interdependent system where value is created by the whole, not the parts. It's not enough to address each element in turn and hope that the sum becomes greater than the parts. The parts must be made to work together constructively. It is like trying to play chess in three dimensions or perform a symphony in several keys at once. It's not surprising, then, that many companies lack the know-how and, consequently, the will to even attempt it.

From the dawn of man until 1954, no one had ever run a mile in under four minutes. It was often thought to be physiologically impossible. In the year after Roger Bannister's record performance, thirty-seven more runners were suddenly able to to it. In the very next year, another 300 runners did the same thing. Today, even some high school runners run a mile in under four minutes.

When everyone in the group is underperforming—when no one is achieving at optimal levels of performance—then the very best becomes relative not to what is achievable but to what has been attained. When the best performance is mediocre, then the best is in fact the most mediocre of them all.

And so to the enigma under evaluation here. The simple truth is that senior executives underperform their companies' potential by 40 percent because they can, because everyone else does, and because shareholders and analysts and customers don't know they're doing it.

To venture after the 40 percent would be the ultimate act of self-exposure. Yet these senior executives have admitted that the prize is there. And imagine what would happen if the bar were universally raised. Imagine if just one of them ran a mile in under four minutes.

A story about the U.S. Navy some hundred years ago illustrates the breakthrough performance that can be achieved when there is a change-agent to provide the *how* and a strong leader who possesses the *will*. The story also offers insight into the principles underlying the successful orchestration of interdependent parts into a whole that produces far more value than the existing system—in this case, 3,000 percent more value.

Teddy Roosevelt and the Enigma of Naval Artillery

"In any moment of decision, the best thing you can do is the right thing, the next best thing is the wrong thing, and the worst thing you can do is nothing."

—THEODORE ROOSEVELT, U.S. PRESIDENT

In the early years of the twentieth century, President Theodore Roosevelt transformed the U.S. Navy. By taking a systems approach to managing and to measuring the value produced by the organization, he was able to achieve a spectacular improvement of 3,000 percent in the accuracy of its artillery—and this at a time when the U.S. Navy's gunners were already considered as accurate as any in the world.

The agent of this change was a young naval officer named William Sowden Sims. It was Sims, with his penetrating insights about the nature of interdependent systems, who lighted the path forward by providing new, more efficient systems. It was Roosevelt, with his indomitable will, who led a reluctant organization down that path and to a level of performance previously unimaginable (see Exhibit 1-5).

A century ago, aiming a gun on the high seas was a clumsy affair. The gun, the target, and the seas all around were in constant motion. Ship's navigators were the heroes in naval combat. They adroitly maneuvered their ships so that the gunners might have a somewhat better chance of hitting their targets.

Meanwhile, British gunners had improved their accuracy simply by adjusting the way they targeted and fired. On maneu-

Exhibit 1-5 – Theodore Roosevelt (left). Admiral William S. Sims (right).

vers in the China Seas, Sims noticed the improvements and wondered if they could be implemented on American ships and even improved further. At the time, naval artillery required only some simple technology. A crank elevated the gun to its proper trajectory for firing shells the full 1,600 yards of its range. A sighting telescope mounted on the barrel enabled the gunner to keep a fix on the target—until just before the firing recoil.

Sims reasoned that moving the sight from the barrel meant that the gun's recoil would no longer affect the gunner, who formerly was forced to lose sight of the target at a critical moment. Sims's innovation would enable continuous aim firing, which was likely to produce far greater accuracy. To compensate for the height and timing of the ship's roll, Sims proposed adjusting the gear ratios so that the gunner could easily raise and lower a gun to follow a target through all the motions of the ship.

Sims calculated that his modifications could increase accuracy by over 3,000 percent without additional cost, technology, or manpower. His superiors ignored him. Over a two-year period, he wrote a dozen letters to the Navy's top officers, imploring them to listen to him for the good of the organization. The letters went unheeded.

It was, in short, an enigma. Artillery was crucially important for success in battle, yet the Navy's leaders remained uninterested in improving it. How could such a value-laden proposition have so little support? As we have found with corporations, there were other related enigmas as well. The goal of the organization was to maintain naval superiority, yet the organization itself hindered that strategy. Dominated by navigators up and down the line, the Navy's navigator "executives" believed that their narrow skill was the great differentiator in battle, not the orchestration of gun, ship, and manpower into an integrated interdependent war fighting system (Exhibit 1-6).

Sims sent his thirteenth letter to President Theodore Roosevelt, the commander-in-chief. A hero of the Spanish-American war and a commander well versed in military matters, Roosevelt

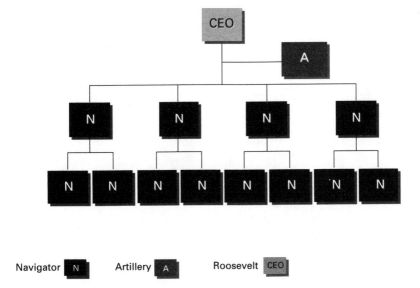

Exhibit 1-6 – Navigators dominated the U.S. Navy's organization in 1900.

was ideally suited to appreciate the significance of Sims's proposal. He recognized the breakthrough potential of Sims's system, but he also recognized that he would personally have to see the change through himself if it was to have any chance of success. He also understood that no military organization could risk complacency.

Roosevelt responded immediately, writing to Sims and ordering his report to be distributed to every officer in the U.S. Navy. Progress was slow at first, but with Roosevelt's vigorous backing, Sims's innovations were implemented. By 1902, the gains in accuracy were precisely as Sims had predicted: 3,000 percent! Continuous-aim firing soon changed the entire U.S. Navy and eventually every navy in the world (Exhibit 1-7).

How vast was that improvement? During the Spanish-American

Exhibit 1-7 – By 1902, "continuous aim firing" had improved accuracy by 3,000 percent.

War in 1898, the U.S. Navy fired a total of 9,500 shells. Only 121 of these shells—1.3 percent—hit anything at all. In 1899, the Navy conducted an exhibition target practice. For twenty-five minutes gunners fired at a target ship from a distance of approximately one mile. They registered exactly two hits and those were only to the sails of the target ship. Yet, a scant three years later, the U.S. gunners hit a similar target ship every time they fired; half of the shells hit a 50-inch square.

Interestingly, the Navy's hit-rate of 1.3 percent, which we would regard as abysmal today, was considered good enough in 1898. Improvement appeared either too difficult or too costly. Yet Roosevelt improved performance by 3,000 percent without new technology, without additional manpower, and without additional cost. All of the elements for a high-performing system were already in place. It simply remained for someone to make all of those elements work together to produce maximum value.

Sims's and Roosevelt's solving of the enigma of naval artillery performance offers some instructive lessons for solving the enigma of corporate value:

- A systems approach produced breakthrough performance improvement. Roosevelt and Sims succeeded because they had the vision to understand that it was the system as an interdependent group of elements forming the whole that produced the value.
- Measuring the system as a whole improved the performance of the whole. Instead of measuring only the accuracy of individual gunners or the prowess of individual navigators, Sims measured the accuracy of the system.
- Factoring in the risk of the alternatives provided a basis for sound decision making. Roosevelt understood that embarking on what appeared to be sweeping change entailed far less risk than failing to improve the Navy's woeful accuracy, no matter how good the Navy believed it to be.

■ Maximum efficiency required effective management of the Navy's asset portfolios—its men, their skills, its weapons, and its ships. Never again would the ships and navigators take precedence over the guns and the gunners, but all would be managed as an integrated weapons-delivery system.

■ The organization changed to match the strategy. In the years following his initial innovations, Sims redirected the course of navy training and retooling. Changing the way naval combat was conceived ultimately required organizational change in the Navy itself.

Solving the Enigma

"The significant problems we face cannot be solved at the same level of thinking we were at when we created them."

—ALBERT EINSTEIN, AMERICAN PHYSICIST

The story of Sims and Roosevelt contains, in embryonic form, the principles of the solution to the 40 percent gap. Based on years of working with hundreds of major companies and of working closely with senior executives in proprietary seminars and academic settings, we have found that those principles apply at any level of the organization: the department, the division, the business unit, and the corporate levels. Those principles may be stated and, more importantly, put into action as a series of five rules:

Rule 1: Manage value as a system.
Rule 2: Measure the system, not the components.
Rule 3: Quantify risk in developing strategy.
Rule 4: Move all asset portfolios onto their "efficient frontier."
Rule 5: Design your organization as the vision of an "optimized future state."

Interestingly, the first of these rules applies to the systems approach as a whole, and each of the succeeding four rules applies to one of the four interdependent elements of the system: business strategy, asset portfolios, financial measures and structure, and organization and operations. By applying the five rules systematically and concurrently, executives can capture that 40 percent in additional value that they *know* is out there—and maximize the value of their organizations.

Rule One: Manage Value as a System

Word-class athletes in golf, tennis, and swimming perform basically the same operations as do novices in each of these sports. The swing, the serve, the stroke are common to elite and novice athlete alike. The difference is not size, not strength, nor the knowledge of the rules. The difference is systems performance: how the interdependent parts work in concert to optimize the performance of the whole.

Elite golfers, tennis players, and swimmers are more efficient and effective than the novice or average player. In golf, as an example, the elite player covers the same ground in fewer strokes and in less time than the novice. The professional is quicker and better because he concentrates on the system.

We're accustomed to thinking about many kinds of systems in a company—information technology, communications, manufacturing, incentives, and numerous others. Rarely, do we think of value as a system. Yet that is what the corporation is—or should be: a vast system of interdependent components working together to produce value.

To address the four components of value—business strategy, asset portfolios, financial measures and structure, and organization and operations—as a system, we have to think about their growth and relationship to each other. We must understand and design the components and linkages from the perspective of the overall system—concurrently and systematically, not separately and sequentially. Optimal value is created through the systematic growth of these four components together, although they sometimes change and grow at different rates (Exhibit 1-8).

Each of these interdependent elements is a means to an end, not an end in itself.

- A business strategy—when correctly developed—clearly identifies the optimal value destination and the best road to get there; it identifies value, it does not produce it.
- Asset portfolios are a collection of business units, divisions, equipment, intellectual property, and people, which are filled with potential value; how to get the best short-term return while creating maximum long-term value is the key.

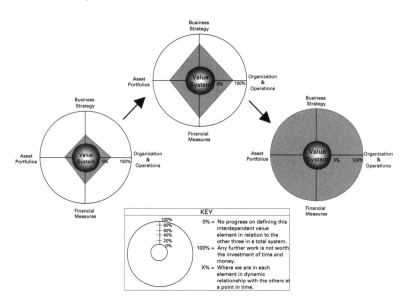

Exhibit 1-8 – Optimal value is created through the systematic growth of business strategy, asset portfolios, financial measures and structure, and organization and operations.

- Financial measures are plentiful and readily available; the key is what to measure, where, when, and how.
- Organization and operations are the engine to run on the road to strategy; too often the engine is not a Rolls Royce jet, but a rubber band.

It is difficult to make advances in strategy without thinking about organizational and operational change. Organizational change requires the optimization of the asset portfolios and a hard look at financial measures that integrate and measure the value that is produced. Such an approach doesn't absolutely guarantee success, but it does guarantee that everything that can possibly be done has been done to secure that additional 40 percent in value.

Of the original 500 companies we surveyed, 70 percent do not address the four components of value concurrently and systematically. They address only some of these components concurrently, or they address them all sequentially or separately (Exhibit 1-9). (According to an online survey of an additional 300 executives in 2002, 99 percent reported not addressing the four value components concur concurrently and systematically.) This fragmented decision making, as the executives recognize, is responsible for much of the value left on the table.

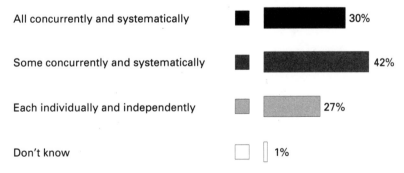

All concurrently and systematically	30%
Some concurrently and systematically	42%
Each individually and independently	27%
Don't know	1%

Exhibit 1-9 – When thinking about corporate performance and value, how do executives consider the four value system components?

Rule Two: Measure the System, Not the Components

Most organizations measure the components of value, not the entire system. To gauge the quality and the value of a business strategy, organizations typically use the net present value of discounted cash flow, or internal rate of return. To track the effectiveness of assets, they use such measures as capacity, utilization, and return on assets. To measure financial performance, they typically rely on measures such as return on equity and earnings before interest, taxes, depreciation, and amortization (EBITDA). To assess organizational operations, they use numerous measures of processes and productivity (Exhibit 1-10).

That is a lot of measurement. Much of it is useful and necessary, but few organizations employ a single overriding financial measure that integrates other financial measures and tracks the performance of the entire system of value. Understanding the inadequacy of unintegrated measures, many organizations implement executive dashboards or balanced scorecards. Used properly, a balanced scorecard can provide useful insight about the

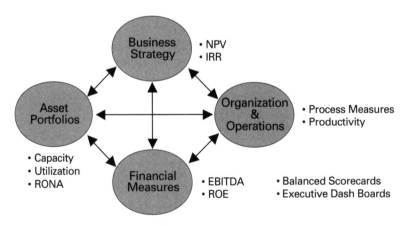

Exhibit 1-10 – Most organizations measure the components of value, not the system.

performance of the system as a system, at least in part. Unfortunately, many organizations implement balanced scorecards as a collection of measures rather than as an integrated measurement system, or they choose inappropriate measures. As a result, the balanced scorecard simply repeats the fundamental error it was originally designed to correct.

Given that more than 70 percent of companies in our research do not address the four components of value concurrently and systematically, it's hardly surprising that most companies do not use integrated financial measures. If a company is doing things separately and sequentially, it's likely to measure them that way. We found that only 6 percent of companies employ an integrated set of financial measures with one primary measure (Exhibit 1-11). The fact that 30 percent of companies practice rule one—*approach value as a system*—but only 6 percent use appropriate financial measures, underscores the necessity of thoroughly practicing each rule. No matter how well intentioned, systematic approaches to value that fail to measure the financial performance of the system *as a system* are likely to produce disappointing results.

The key to rule two is to apply a system-level value-based measure to drive the performance of the overall system. There are a number of such value-based measures that might be used.

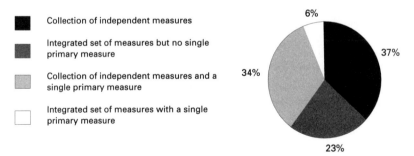

Collection of independent measures

Integrated set of measures but no single primary measure

Collection of independent measures and a single primary measure

Integrated set of measures with a single primary measure

6%

37%

34%

23%

Exhibit 1-11 – Executives' responses to the question: "Which statement best describes performance measurement in your organization?"

For example, it's possible to measure net present value of cash flows across all four components of the system and then measure the whole in those terms. *Economic value-added* (EVA) is another value-based measure that can be usefully applied to each of the four components of the system and used to integrate measurement of the whole. Both of these measures share three key characteristics: They are value-based, they are system level, and they are capable of integrating the measures of the four components of the system. In a recent study, we found that over 50 percent of corporations do use common profit measures and internal rate of return, but they do not use specific value-based metrics.

Rule Three: Quantify Risk in Developing Strategy

Nearly 50 percent of executives report that to achieve full value, it is critical to understand the relationship between creating value and taking risk. In fact, we found that every company claims to weigh risk in some fashion or other. But only 26 percent explicitly identify sources of risk and uncertainty and measure them quantitatively (Exhibit 1-12). This is like what happens in dieting—you know what you need to do, but you're just not doing it.

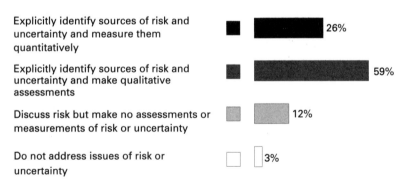

Explicitly identify sources of risk and uncertainty and measure them quantitatively — 26%

Explicitly identify sources of risk and uncertainty and make qualitative assessments — 59%

Discuss risk but make no assessments or measurements of risk or uncertainty — 12%

Do not address issues of risk or uncertainty — 3%

Exhibit 1-12 – Executives' responses to the question: "In making strategic decisions in your organizations, what best describes how you account for risk and uncertainty?"

Rule Four: Move All Asset Portfolios onto Their Efficient Frontier

To grasp the significance of rule four, it's necessary to think broadly about what constitutes a portfolio of assets. Corporations have many types of asset portfolios. A corporation that operates several business units could be said to have a portfolio of business units. Within those units, there are functions and business processes, which are also asset portfolios. Products, services, intellectual property, patents, technology, systems applications—the list crosses all aspects of an organization—all are asset portfolios. Physical assets like real estate, plants, and distribution facilities represent yet another kind of portfolio. People can even be thought of as an asset portfolio, which ensures that you're treating people as you should be treating them—as an asset.

The goal is to maximize the expected return on investment in each of these portfolios. Sometimes, however, a given portfolio must be suboptimized to get the most value for the corporation. The key is to align each of the portfolios with the corporation's business strategy, financial measures and structure, and organization and operations in order to maximize overall shareholder value.

To bring about the concurrent growth of all of the interdependent parts of the value system—and close the 40 percent gap in value—all of these asset portfolios must be brought onto their efficient frontier. For many, "efficient frontier" is an unfamiliar concept. To understand it, consider mutual funds. An investment in a mutual fund is an investment in a portfolio, which could include anything from low-risk, low-return CDs up to high-risk, high-return investments in emerging markets, but the investor's ultimate risk and return comes from the performance of the entire portfolio. A portfolio is on the efficient frontier when the portfolio maximizes return (or benefit) for a given level of risk (or cost). Chapter 3 will discuss this topic in detail.

Exhibit 1-13 illustrates, in simplified fashion, a set of portfolios and their relation to the efficient frontier. The graph measures short-term, current year earnings against long-term value creation for each of the portfolios. Portfolio A is yielding big returns in terms of current year earnings, but it is unlikely to create much long-term value. At the other end of the spectrum, Portfolio G is garnering little in current year earnings but is likely to create a great deal of long-term value. Portfolio D and Portfolio E yield the same in current earnings, but Portfolio D promises far more long-term value. Faced with the choice of these two portfolios, any rational person would choose Portfolio D every time. In this case, a portfolio is on the efficient frontier when it is in the best long-term position for any given level of current earnings. Other kinds of portfolios would of course require other kinds of measures, but in the end those measures will be financial.

For most companies, the performance of their asset portfolios is less than efficient. On average, executives report that they are

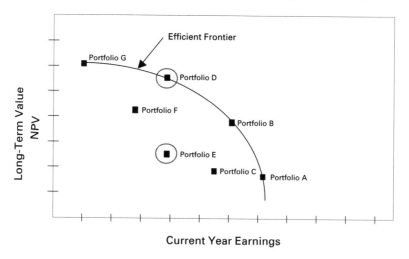

Exhibit 1-13 – Rule Four: Move all asset portfolios onto their efficient frontier.

getting less than 70 percent of the potential value of their assets. On average, the executives also say that they should divest 20 percent of the corporation's assets because those assets are worth more to someone else than to their own organization (Exhibit 1-14).

This underperformance points to the first step in applying the concept of the efficient frontier: Get on it in the first place. That means getting all of the asset portfolios of all kinds onto their corresponding efficient frontier. The second step is to optimize the placement of the portfolios on the current efficient frontier. Then it's possible to begin to move them around, explore trade-offs, and put them fully at the service of the organization's strategic and financial goals. The third step is to move onto a new efficient frontier. By looking to external opportunities, it's possible to push the efficient frontier outward (Exhibit 1-15).

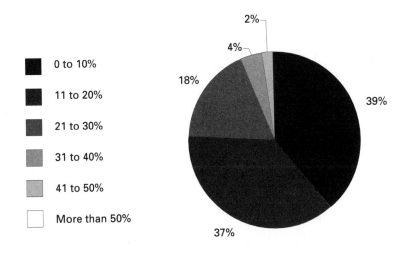

Exhibit 1-14 – Executives' responses to the question: "What percentage of your corporation's assets should be divested because the assets are worth more to another corporation?"

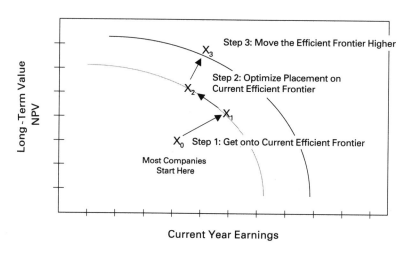

Exhibit 1-15 – Getting on the efficient frontier is only the first step.

Rule Five: Design the Organization as the Vision of an Optimized Future State

To design the current organization as it would look in an optimized future state, you must first envision that future. Most organizations can see ahead, with some clarity, about three to five years. What should your organization look like then? How should it be performing? What place will it occupy in the market? Develop a clear vision of that state and commit the organization to it. If you don't know where you're going, you'll never get there: The journey is not the destination. The destination is the destination.

Second, you must understand the current state of the organization. Where are we now—today? This is not as straightforward as it seems. Often, what emerges is striking disagreement, at all levels, on precisely what that current state is.

Third, begin devising paths that will take the organization from its current state to its "to be" state. In effect, you're crossing the gap between today and that destination three or five years down the road.

This is hard but necessary work, especially when it's being done concurrently with work on business strategy, financial measures, and asset portfolios, as it must be. Some 68 percent of the executives reported that their organizational structure impeded their strategy. (Exhibit 1-16). The structure was not simply unhelpful, it hindered the ability of the organization to create and deliver value. The executives also reported a 25 percent gap between their existing organizational structures and the organizational structure they needed. In addition, fully half of the executives surveyed said that their organizations handled change poorly. Of that half, 50 percent said that their organizations handled change disastrously.

These are real measures of how challenging rule five can be. Not only do these executives say that their organizations' business strategy, asset portfolios, and financial measures and structure are misaligned, but that they would have real difficulty in making the necessary changes to achieve alignment.

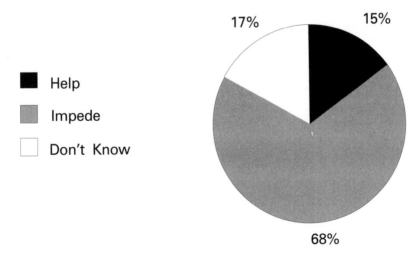

Exhibit 1-16 – Executives' responses to the question: "Does your organization help or impede the implementation of your strategy?"

Applying the Rules

Applying all five rules concurrently is no easy task. But the reward can be enormous, since as much as 40 percent of value goes untapped by the typical organization.

How do organizations get started? First, they size the value gap. How big is the prize? Although the average size of the value gap among our 500 companies is 40 percent, in many of those companies the gap was as much as 70 percent. Rewards of that magnitude provide a powerful incentive for action. Second, they diagnose the misalignment in strategy, assets, financial measures and structures, and organization and operations. Third, they prove the concept through a turbo pilot—a value system project first tested at the department or division level. Then they roll it out to the entire organization and let the enthusiasm spread.

This bare-bones outline of the five rules and the steps toward implementing them inadequately conveys where the real power of the approach lies—and that is in its details. From the time of Teddy Roosevelt down to today, both before and after the recession, 9/11, and Enron's collapse, the basics of business haven't changed. Neither have the problems. What about the solution? In the largest sense, it hasn't changed since the time of Frederick Taylor: Put back together what, for the sake of efficiency and productivity, has to be first broken apart.

What has changed is the availability of powerful conceptual and practical tools for implementing the solution and our understanding of them: How uncertainty in strategy can be quantified with far more precision, how managing portfolios goes far beyond simply rationalizing the assets in them, what various financial measures can and can't do for performance, and what organizational structures work best for which strategies. Most important, we have a far more nuanced and powerful systems approach to all of these interdependent components of value. Succeeding chapters explore each of these issues in detail and elaborate on these rules for addressing them. The god is in the details, as Descartes said. With a firm grasp of those details, the reader should be ready to solve the enigma of corporate value. All that remains is the will.

So how do you do it? How do you solve the corporate value enigma? The solution to the corporate value enigma resides in understanding the five rules and applying them to the interdependent components of value described here. In the next four chapters, we will delve into each of the components of the underlying value system: business strategy, asset portfolios, financial measures and structure, and organization and operations. As always, we start with strategy.

Notes

1. Frederick W. Taylor introduced time-and-motion studies to systematize shop management and reduce manufacturing costs at the Midvale Steel Company in the 1880s.

Starting with Strategy

CHAPTER TWO

"Long range planning does not deal
with future decisions but with the future
of present decisions."

—PETER F. DRUCKER, MANAGEMENT THINKER AND AUTHOR

The worst kept secret in the telecommunications industry is that AT&T is dying. CEO C. Michael Armstrong's strategy of splitting AT&T into separate wireless, cable, and telephone companies appears to be expediting the death of an American icon. The brand name will probably survive; but the institution it once was will not. Did Armstrong and his executive team have a clear understanding of the value and risks in their strategy? Were significantly different yet compelling alternative strategies considered by his team to ensure that the chosen strategy was truly the best path forward in risk versus return? Did they understand the impact of their strategy on the many and varied asset portfolios at AT&T's command? Could the organization and corporate culture adapt to the requirements of the split-up strategy? Were the balance sheets of these separate companies powerful enough to absorb the changes required by such a split-up?

All of these questions are relevant and must be answered when constructing strategy. This chapter will chart the way through strategy development and the required alignment of business strategy with asset portfolios, financial structures and measures, and organization and operations. We begin with Alpha Forest Products, an example company that will appear throughout the book to illustrate the successful application of these principles.

CASE STUDY

Introducing Alpha Forest Products

Alpha Forest Products—which will be referred to as AFP throughout the book—has been a leading company in the paper, wood, packaging, and related fields for more than a century. In the 1990s, the company found itself underperforming compared with its competitors in the industry as well as with manufacturing companies in the wood sector as a whole. The business had always been cyclical and issues of price and capacity had long been seen as the driving forces that determined profitability and growth. In fact, many people at AFP took those factors to be immutable laws of their business. But not the new, innovative executive team. They decided to take their fate in their own hands.

AFP's senior executive leadership team certainly didn't have all the answers, but they had the foresight to seek a new way to ask the questions. They started with one of the enigmas of corporate performance that many corporations—including their own—couldn't even cover the cost of their capital. Why not just sell the corporation's assets and invest the money? That was a question asked more than once. But the deeper enigma for AFP, as for this book, was why anyone would *want* a business where the return would not surpass the cost of capital needed to run that business. And there was a further enigma—the conventional wisdom that said "it is what it is" and nothing could change it.

How to extricate AFP from century-old conventional wisdom? AFP, like many of its competitors in the field, has fourth and fifth generation family members working for it. The products are old and well established; the factories are, for the most part, old and tired; and investor attention, especially in the 1990s, was focused elsewhere.

AFP's management team was undaunted. They refused to be deterred by the challenge of organizational intractability, the hoary precepts of conventional wisdom, or the dip in the cyclical market in which they found themselves. In the face of so many obstacles, many companies wouldn't dare to act. But inspired by evidence that the best time to invest was in the "trough," AFP's management team moved forward.

They sought to build on the company's earlier work in quality, in reengineering, in strategic applications of information technology, in incentives and financial measures, and in change management. AFP's breakthrough came when they began to really see how deeply their direction, their assets, their operations, and their finances were all interconnected and interdependent. Seeing business strategy, asset portfolios, finances, and organization and operations as interdependent parts of a unified whole emboldened the team to make great changes.

From 1992 to1997, the company was in the bottom-tier of its industry with a below-average total shareholder return compared to its competitors. In 1995, they began to apply the *five rules* in earnest. They rapidly went from being a bottom tier performer to industry leader, measured in total shareholder return.

Alpha Forest Products Asks the Right Strategic Questions

The epiphany for AFP came in a meeting where it was decided to look hard at each of the current businesses and determine the sources and magnitudes of value and risk in each of the businesses, and not to consider them all as part of a greater low margin, commodity business. A quantitative, alternatives-based approach to strategy was required for each business area. Tough questions were proposed and a commitment was forged to get down to the honest-to-God's truth of the prospects for each of these businesses.

- What are the high margin products and services that AFP could refocus their resources on?
- Which assets would be required to pursue the higher margin offerings?
- What performance measures would drive decisions and actions toward improved financial performance?
- What are the characteristics of an organization and operations to drive all of the needed changes and sustain them once achieved?

All of these questions were placed on the executives' table. On that day in 1995, AFP started down a much improved path in developing a corporate strategy. The approach itself was a breakthrough in that for decades prior to this day, AFP had waffled back and forth between two typical frames for corporate strategy development: an inside-out approach and an outside-in approach.

The Solution Is in the Room

It is 7:00 P.M. on a Thursday evening in Company A's corporate conference room. Strewn across the long mahogany table are Madison Avenue quality presentation packages from the various corporate business units detailing market opportunities, required investments, financial forecasts, and action plans for success. A closed, thick, black binder containing competitor analyses lies in the middle of the table riddled with yellow stickies, marking relevant factoids that must be considered in the heroic exercise of constructing the corporation's strategy.

In a corporate strategy meeting earlier that week, one of the senior executives had tugged the elbow of an observer and quietly told him, "You have just witnessed one of our strongest core competencies, the internal marketing and selling of business plans by our business unit heads." He was right. Through the succeeding three days the observer listened to the business unit leaders present their proposed business unit strategies. Each presentation was well prepared and presented. The presentation documents were of the highest quality featuring high-quality graphics, color, flow, and overall layout. And the financial projections were just as stunning and positive. Unfortunately, the financial projections did not jibe with the business units' past performance, implying a near-term, significant discontinuity in the corporation's financial performance. This would be great if it were believable. It was not.

The vice president of corporate strategy had been given the simple directive from the CEO that the company had to be first or second in each of its markets or get out. The business unit heads had done a great job of defining, and in many cases redefining, their markets to ensure that their current market positioning was first or second. Now, the vice president of corporate strategy was attempting to construct a coherent corporate story on how to place bets among these disparate business units to win big in the marketplace. The solution was somewhere in the room, somewhere in the collection of the week's conversations that were held among the corporate executives and business unit leaders. Or was it?

The Solution Is Outside the Room

A different company, a different scenario: It is 9:00 A.M. on a Monday morning. Company B's executives have gathered in the CEO's private conference room to prepare for the discussion they'll be having with the CEO on the corporation's strategy. Suddenly, the door flies open and in struts a man on a mission, the CEO. After the briefest of introductions, the CEO steps to an enclosed white board and opens it up to reveal his detailed notes on the corporate strategy. He begins by stating, "I started with a clean sheet." "My executive team just isn't thinking broadly enough." "They're stuck in the past." For the next thirty minutes he holds forth on how he plans to position and rebuild the corporation. He is animated, energized, and full to the brim with conviction about the soundness of his plan.

The entire game plan does sound striking, and certainly looks like a recipe for success. At the end of his monologue, the CEO explains his need—to get commitment and alignment from his executive team and their organizations. He also needs them to detail an implementation plan for executing his vision. For this CEO, the solution comes from outside the room, outside the universe of visions and perspectives of his executive team. The current state of the corporation had little to do with the future he had envisioned. In his mind, the only obstacle to success would be the executive team's failure to execute.

These two situations occurred several years ago. In both cases the corporations failed to create any significant shareholder value and both companies have less than stellar corporate reputations. These two situations represent opposite ends of a spectrum in strategic perspective: a bubble-up, inside-out perspective and a top-down, outside-in perspective. Corporations tend toward one or the other end of the spectrum, rarely striking a good balance, and it's usually easy to identify where on the spectrum a corporation falls when it comes to corporate strategy. Also, although these two corporations shared similar weak financial performances, they differed in at least one dimension—the potential corporate value identified in their strategies. The bottom-up approach identified little of the potential corporate value due to its overwhelmingly incremental perspective on possibilities and change. The top-down approach identified a significant percentage of the potential corporate value, but it inevitably became a bridge too far. Exhibit 2-1 summarizes and compares these different strategic perspectives to approaching strategy development.

Senior executives believe that, on average, their organization's strategies identify about 75 percent of the potential value of their organization.[1] And one out of ten senior executives believes their strategies identify 50 percent or less of the organization's potential value. It has been common knowledge for years that a pure bubble-up strategy will never uncover the hidden value of a corporation with a portfolio of businesses. It has become equally apparent that a pure "clean sheet" approach to corporate strategy is fraught with implementation risk and more often than not results in a hit-and-miss execution that does not

	Solution Is in the Room (Bubble-Up Corporate Strategy)	Solution Is Outside the Room (Clean-Sheet Corporate Strategy)	Value System Approach to Corporate Strategy
Given	• Financial Structure —Balance Sheet —Capital Budget • Majority of Assets Fixed • Operations/Organization	• Not much	• Not much
Focus	• Markets • Products and Services • Market and Distribution Channels • Capital Allocation	• Potentially anything	• Potentially anything • Impact and changes to asset portfolios • Impact and changes in financial structure • Impact and changes to operations and organization
Expected Result	• Incremental improvements —Financial —Efficiency	• Pockets of significant improvement both top and bottom line • Most of the organization is left unchanged due to inability to implement • Significant gap between value potential and value captured	• Systematic significant improvement in top and bottom line • Significant reduction in gap between value potential and value captured

Exhibit 2-1 – Perspectives on approaching strategy development.

guarantee that the company will capture the majority of the potential value. Having stated the obvious, the question remains, how do you balance and account for the corporation's asset portfolios, financial measures and structure, and organization and operations when creating corporate strategy without getting lost in the details?

Strategy Is One Component of a Value System

As we have seen, our research found that about 70 percent of organizations do not concurrently and systematically address their four components of value. Although virtually all of the executives we surveyed believe that they could increase shareholder value by aligning these components, more than 20 percent of the executives polled believe they could improve the financial performance of their company by 50 percent or more. With this much at stake, why don't senior executives align these four components? What can be done to ensure alignment across these components? First, consider the essence of the four components that must be aligned:

■ *Business Strategy.* A corporation's strategy and business model consist of the decisions that determine the customer value chain they choose to participate in and the position of the business within that value chain.

■ *Asset Portfolios.* Every business is made up of several portfolios, such as business units, markets, products and services, functions, business processes, facilities, technologies, intellectual property, R&D, and even people. Divesting these assets can unlock the capital required for the changes the organization should be pursuing but currently can't afford to make.

■ *Financial Measures and Structure.* What financial performance measures should we be using to motivate behaviors, improve decisions, and drive actions? How can we ensure that shareholder value is a primary measure that other subordinate measures drive? Largely the role of the finance department, the decisions and actions within the financial structure are capital-focused. Do we need to restructure our debt to position ourselves better for our strategy and future business model? Do we need additional capital and if so, what are the sources we should be considering? What level of funding do we need to pursue the changes we need to make? Should we consider establishing an internal venture capital organization?

■ *Operations and Organization.* The focus here is on the efficiency of operations and, as importantly, the capability to change with respect to changes in each of the other three value system components. What change initiatives should we be pursuing, canceling, postponing, or redesigning? Do we have the right individuals leading our change initiatives? Are our change initiatives sufficiently coordinated? Do we need to improve the governance and communications within and across our change initiatives?

Although senior executives agree that aligning the decisions and actions across these four components is key to getting more value, how to do it remains an enigma for most.

Why Is It So Difficult to Align the Four Components of a Value System?

There are many reasons why it is difficult to align the decisions and actions across a corporation's business strategy, portfolio of assets, financial measures and structure, and organization and operations. Here are the seven most fundamental issues and problems.

■ *The responsibilities and accountabilities of the decisions and actions reside in separate parts of the organization, with no formal mechanism to ensure alignment.* In most organizations, strategy is the work of the CEO, the business unit leaders, and the strategic planning organization. The CFO and the finance department have accountability for all capital and debt matters. The COO has accountability for operations with equivalent roles accountable at the business unit level. The various portfolios (business units, markets, products, business processes, facilities, technologies, intellectual property, R&D, and people) typically have the weakest accountabilities due to their spread throughout organizations. With such a wide network of accountabilities, it is clear that a formal mechanism must be in place to ensure alignment let alone optimization.

■ *No means exist to pinpoint and measure the value and risks within and across the four components of the value system.* How can you make good trade-offs in decision making if you are not measuring the costs, benefits, and risks associated with these interrelated decisions? Most organizations use value measures, such as economic value added (EVA), net present value (NPV) of discounted cash flow, ROI, and IRR, to evaluate their strategies. Few use these measures consistently in decisions across the other three components of the value system. And an even much smaller minority of organizations explicitly accounts for risk. Yet *optimizing* the decisions across all four components to maximize value requires just this: using a consistent value measure or set of measures across all four components and a comprehensive and quantitative perspective on risk.

■ *Strategic decision-making in the organization is an advocacy process as opposed to a learning process.* Most organizations use a scientific method-like approach to making decisions. They create a hypothesis and then collect information and data to support or refute the hypothesis. Unfortunately, the information and data that gets to the table for discussion is usually that which supports the hypothesis—hence termed an advocacy process. During reviews of these strategic decisions, senior executives spend their energy attempting to shoot holes in the hypothesis and the supporting information. In the best case, if the hypothesis and supporting information survive the senior executive discussion, a decision is made.

The problem with such a process is that significantly different alternatives are not pursued or discussed. How would you know whether the initial hypothesis is the best alternative? No other significantly different alternatives were ever truly considered. Learning about what is more valuable and what is less valuable only comes through examination of significantly different alternatives. Moreover, strategic-level decisions in any of the four value system components must include consideration of each of the other three components of the value system.

■ *Individual incentives are not aligned with the decisions and actions required to maximize value.* Examples of this are easy to find in any organization. Consider a call center where individuals are rated by the volume of calls they handle during a shift, or a manufacturing line where workers are rated by the number of widgets they assemble per week, or regional sales managers who are rated by the total number of sales their region make in a quarter. In each of these cases, volume is the underlying rating, and in each of these cases volume is probably not a good indicator of sustainable profitability or shareholder value creation.

■ *No explicit activity is in place to ensure the alignment and commitment of individuals to the decisions and actions required to maximize value.* How often in your organization is a decision made, yet several weeks later it is clear that there has been insufficient action taken to implement the decision? The decision makers were committed to the decision but the implementers were not. Building commitment to action is a process, not an event. The sheer declaration of a decision rarely ensures its implementation. Getting sufficient commitment to implement change requires work and a plan—and not just a communication plan, but an alignment plan.

■ *The organization doesn't know how to measure or judge the quality of many strategic decisions that have uncertain outcomes and long time horizons.* Most operational decisions and strategic decisions differ in at least one fundamental way—the time required to get feedback on the outcome of the decision. The result or outcome of a strategic decision may not be apparent for years and, in some industries, decades. Further, strategic decisions typically entail far more uncertainty than operational decisions. Consequently, the quality of a strategic decision cannot be measured by its outcome; something else must be used to judge its quality. The best you can do for decisions with long time horizons and uncertainty is to maximize the probability of getting a good outcome. Consequently, the goal of a strategic decision-making process should be just that.

■ *The organization doesn't know where or how to get started in aligning the four value system components*. Aligning the four value system components is complex. It's fraught with uncertainty caused by changes in markets and competition, by world events, and by political turmoil; and these are just the external sources. The internal workings of a corporation carry their own usual myriad of issues, challenges, and uncertainties. On the surface, it seems overwhelming to consider optimizing, let alone aligning, the four components. Like losing weight, the hurdles are getting started and then sticking with the program.

Decision Quality Is the Key

Strategy is ultimately a decision-making process. Making high quality decisions is the goal of any decision-making process in an organization. High quality strategic decisions share six common elements:

1. *Appropriate Frame:* Having an appropriate decision frame means that you are focusing on the right decision(s) and that your perspective is broad enough and insightful. It's crucial that decision makers agree on what is given, on what is out-of-scope or to be addressed later, and on what is in focus. In short, what are the specific decisions that will be addressed? For a clear and simple example of the need for an appropriate frame, consider the way spouses make decisions about their home. What starts out as a discussion about whether to re-carpet leads to discussions about whether to postpone the carpeting because of the need for a new room addition, which leads to a discussion about whether to sell their home and move to a bigger one. That progression of topics includes at least three different decision frames. The lesson is clear: You need to decide on what you are going to decide.

2. *Clear Value and Trade-Offs:* Being clear on value and trade-offs means that you understand the sources and magnitudes of value from the perspectives of the key stakeholders, and that you understand the relationships and trade-offs among these perspectives. The first question to ask is "Who are the stakeholders and what do they want?" That is a simple, but powerful, question. Answering both of its parts will drive much of the work in achieving a high-quality decision. For example, shareholders for an automobile manufacturer want shareholder value growth, union leaders want good jobs with safe working environments, the EPA wants reduced emissions, and consumers want reliable vehicles. Achieving optimal trade-offs across these goals requires explicit understanding and measurement.

3. *Meaningful, Reliable Information:* Having meaningful and reliable information means that you have the information that is relevant to the decisions at hand and that when uncertainty exists in this information it is accounted for explicitly. Recall the vice president of corporate strategy mentioned at the outset of this chapter. He had reams of data, but not necessarily meaningful and decision-relevant data. Knowing what information is needed to support decision making requires knowing what decisions need to be made.

4. *Creative, Doable Alternatives:* Having creative and doable alternatives means that you have considered significantly different courses of action and that several attractive and compelling alternatives have been established. Former Secretary of State Henry Kissinger once tellingly characterized the alternatives his advisors would bring to him for consideration. He complained that the advisors would bring three alternatives—one that would lead to global thermonuclear warfare, one that would lead to the surrender of the United States, and one that the advisory team wanted to pursue. Significantly different, yes; but not compelling.

5. *Correct Reasoning:* Having logically correct reasoning means that you have structured the evaluations of the various alternatives to ensure that they are logically sound and correct. It is of utmost importance that this include logically consistent accounting for uncertainty and risk. Risk and uncertainty form a set of relationships that is too complex to be left to human judgment and qualitative evaluation. Just as a pilot learns to fly from instruments instead of relying on instinct or vision, managing and mitigating risk requires looking at the measurement instruments.

6. *Commitment to Action:* Achieving commitment to action means that you have sufficiently involved the key stakeholders in the decision in order to assure their commitment. Here is an illustration of what happens when commitment to action is not clearly agreed to. As a new executive at General Motors left one of his first meetings where a decision had just been made, a colleague told him, "You just got the GM nod." However, the executive was convinced not only that there was insufficient alignment on that decision, but also that the underlying issues impeding that alignment had not been discussed. As it turned out, he was right. There had been no commitment to actually implement the decision, and the participants in the room who opposed the decision knew that the best defense against it was to let it die on its own through passive resistance. No action was ever taken to implement the decision that appeared to have been made that day in the conference room.

Measuring the quality of a strategic decision can be done by assessing each of the above six elements on a scale of 0 to 100 percent, as illustrated in Exhibit 2-2. A score of 100 percent for any one element means that placing any additional effort on improving the quality of the element would not be worth the effort. A high-quality strategic decision must score well in each of the six elements. Having the key stakeholders in a decision score each of these elements regularly throughout the decision-making process pinpoints the sources of disagreement and concerns and hence determines the focus of future work to achieve a high-quality decision.

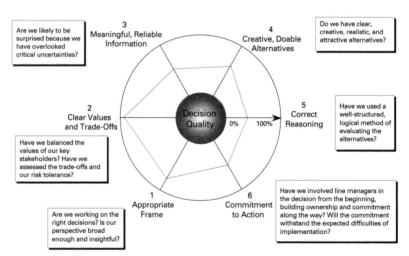

Exhibit 2-2 – The six characteristics of making a high quality strategic decision.

Strategy Must Be Aligned to Asset Portfolios

Chapter 3 details the way to optimize the performance of the many asset portfolios a corporation holds. The question here is how to create a strategy and ensure that the decisions and actions in the strategy are consistent and aligned with the decisions and actions associated with the various asset portfolios.

When constructing a corporate strategy you should consider these questions about asset portfolios:

■ *Which asset portfolios are potentially impacted by the business strategy?* A corporate strategy could potentially impact any of the asset portfolios. Portfolios include business units, markets, products and services, customers, intellectual property, R&D, facilities, competencies, functions, and business processes.

■ *For those asset portfolios potentially impacted, does the strategy significantly alter any of the "core components" of the portfolio or significantly degrade the performance of the portfolio?* As we will discuss in Chapter 3, each asset portfolio has core components. The asset portfolio manager is accountable for sustaining those components and ensuring that the portfolio is performing satisfactorily. If the strategy adversely impacts an asset portfolio, then reconsidering the asset portfolio must become part of the work in developing the corporate strategy.

■ *If the corporate strategy requires a merger, acquisition, or divestiture, what impact does the merger, acquisition, or divestiture have on the associated asset portfolios?* Transactions involving people impact multiple asset portfolios. For example, when east coast defense contractor Raytheon acquired the west coast defense businesses of Hughes Electronics, many asset portfolios came into play. Facilities had to be rationalized, staffs needed to be combined, competing technologies needed to be combined and or eliminated, business processes such as software development needed to be integrated, and business functions such as accounting and human resources needed to be rationalized.

Hughes Electronics had one of the highest-rated software development teams and processes in the country, as assessed by the Software Engineering Institute (SEI) of Carnegie-Mellon University. Keeping that team and capability intact was a high priority for Raytheon since that team, capability, and national rating were keys to winning new business. It would have been easy to argue for the consolidation of the Hughes operations with Raytheon's east coast facilities, but key personnel were unwilling to uproot families and move east. As a result, Raytheon kept some west coast facilities open, which created duplications in several business functions. From an asset portfolio perspective, Raytheon was willing to have less than optimal asset portfolios for facilities and business functions in order to ensure the best possible portfolio of experience and competency, which it considered to be the key to winning large contracts.

■ *Is there an asset portfolio that is missing critical components or is underperforming?* Decisions regarding how to improve the performance of an asset portfolio should be moved up into corporate strategy whenever an asset portfolio is missing critical components or is significantly underperforming.

Strategy Must Be Aligned to Financial Measures and Structure

Over the past few years, there has been an admirable movement to get CFOs more involved with corporate strategy. Strategic planning processes that leave out financial input until late in the process risk producing strategies that the corporation "can't afford." The process of slashing and cutting back the corporate budget to an affordable level too often leaves business units with aggressive goals and targets and seemingly insufficient budgets. A tension is manufactured between the CEO/CFO and the business unit heads, which plays out over the course of the planning cycle. The key is to create a productive tension, not one plagued by second-guessing and unrealistic targets that encourage value-destroying behaviors and actions.

The importance of managing the corporation's balance sheet should be on a par with managing the corporation's cash flow and profitability. There should be an explicit strategy for the corporation's balance sheet that is aligned with the overall corporate strategy. Getting a good return on equity is a primary focus of the CFO. Managing the corporation's balance sheet is the CFO's mechanism for capturing a good return. The CEO and CFO can choose the financial measures that will drive the right behaviors, decisions, and actions throughout the corporation, which will be addressed in Chapter 4.

When constructing and evaluating a corporate strategy, you should consider these questions about the corporation's financial structure and financial measures:

■ *Does any debt need to be restructured to enable execution of strategy or to better position for a new business model?* Considerations of financial restructurings are too often separated from the work of strategy or are, at best, an afterthought. Balance sheet strategy should be a part of strategy development or at least explicitly considered, as will be discussed in Chapter 4.

■ *Are there corporate assets that are worth more to another corporation? Should they be considered for divestment to enable strategic investments and position the balance sheet?* Many corporations are in the habit of acquiring but never divesting of assets. For example, Alpha Forest Products made thirty acquisitions over a two-year period, but did not divest any assets during that time. And a CFO of a major corporation recently confided that his company doesn't do divestitures well and typically ends up trying to sell "the ashes of the business."

The key here is that divestiture is a management tool to optimally position the corporation's balance sheet for the future. Divestiture is not just about selling poorly performing assets. It is a way to make sure that the corporation has the right asset portfolios, as we will discuss further in Chapter 3.

■ *Realistically, is additional capital required? If so, what are the sources for it?* Cash flows and capital requirements are uncertain and should be treated accordingly. Chapter 4 discusses how to consider uncertainty in cash flow and capital requirements and consequently how to determine whether additional capital is needed. Traditional as well as creative means for raising capital are listed in Exhibit 2-3.

Traditional Sources of Capital	Creative Sources of Capital
• Stock issues • Increase in long-term debt to existing capital source • Increase in short-term debt to existing capital source • Increase in accounts payable • Retained earnings	• Divest selected assets —Assets more valuable to another organization than your own —Under-utilized assets • Leverage existing assets/contracts/IP/future cash flow • Establish a corporate venturing organization to manage outside sources of capital • Secure private equity funding/partnerships to launch/grow "spin-off" businesses • Reorganize into discrete units to enable equity positions in new ventures from venture capital, strategic partners, or equity partners

Exhibit 2-3 – Traditional and creative sources of capital.

■ *Do we need to overhaul our financial performance measures to ensure that they are aligned with the strategy and changes we need to pursue? Are the financial performance measures aligned with incentives and compensation?* It is well understood in corporate America that you get what you measure. Unfortunately, the execution of this simple, yet profound, truth lags well behind awareness of it. A pulp and paper mill for Alpha Forest Products drives home this point. Success at the mill had been measured for decades by the amount of pulp and paper that was produced each day. A good day meant that pulp was produced at or near capacity and that paper machines ran at or near full capacity. Downtime in the pulping process or paper-making process was bad. Downtime comes in three forms: scheduled maintenance, changes in pulp or paper produced, or system breakdowns. The pulp and paper mill had mastered scheduled maintenance; there were many old systems and machines used in the pulping and paper-making process, but the preventive maintenance schedule minimized the number of system breakdowns. To keep the processes up and running, the mill minimized the number of pulp and paper changes. But while the mill was cranking out pulp and paper at or near capacity, it was filling railroad cars on the back lot with paper that was not in demand.

A new strategy was called for, which meant a big shift in product mix away from the lower grade, lower margin papers to the high end, smaller volume, higher margin papers. This meant much more down time in the processes due to the changes in pulp and paper produced in a given week. Given the culture of the mill, basing the performance measures on economic value added instead of utilization of equipment and facilities was a major change. As a rule, whenever performance measures are changed, incentives and compensation should be reviewed as well. This was certainly the case at the mill.

Strategy Must Be Aligned to Organization and Operations

Creating a new strategy implies change. And if there is one competency you can count on an organization having, it is the competency to resist change. "Tissue rejection" of new strategies is common among organizations. Staff behaviors range from taking an attitude of "all things must pass, this will too," to diverting efforts until the energy behind the change dissipates, to outright collusion in killing the change. The focus of this book is not on how to create organizational alignment at the level of individuals. The focus is on how to align the organization and operations with the other components of the value system, including strategy, financial measures and structure, and asset portfolios. Corporations, like organisms, constantly evolve and change in many dimensions.

Individuals have two in-boxes on their "mental desktops." One in-box contains all the work that corresponds to their job title, role, and reputation. This is often referred to as the work associated with "my real job." The second in-box contains all the additional work that is assigned on an ad-hoc basis, including participation in projects such as strategy development, change programs, and mergers/acquisitions/divestitures. Few organizations these days have staff with a lot of idle time. In fact, the average workload for individuals has been increasing steadily for many years. For most people, another activity added to the in-box is not a welcome sight.

Many organizations that have been unable to successfully develop and execute strategies or implement change programs suffer from an internal reputation of "we can't get anything done." It is understandable that employees in such environments have grown weary of the "project de jour." They find it hard to muster up the energy and enthusiasm to truly commit to the stack of tasks growing in their second in-box. With this as a common context during strategy development, you must address these questions about the organization and operations:

■ *What strategy and change projects are currently being pursued? Which should you continue to pursue, which should be canceled, and which should be postponed?* It is surprising how many on-going projects there are in organizations. In working with organizations, one of the first things we do is to identify all the on-going relevant projects. For example, at the outset of working with a major automobile manufacturer, we found that the company had over 100 relevant projects in progress! How do you get your arms around that? The answer is: with much perseverance and effort.

We have found that organizations, whether corporations or departments, benefit greatly from creating a *change agenda*, a.k.a. a strategic agenda. The idea is simple. The key leaders of the organization get together and create the menu of projects for the year (or for some other agreed upon period). They decide which they will pursue now, which will be postponed, which will not be done at all, and which will be passed down in the organization to another set of leaders. Depending on the size and complexity of the organization and the number of existing projects, this activity takes anywhere from a couple of days to a couple of weeks.

■ *Are the right individuals leading the strategy and change projects that we currently want to pursue?* Selecting the right individuals to manage and lead strategy projects and strategy implementation or change projects requires understanding the distinction between the different modes of management and leadership. Strategy development is a *creative* process; strategy implementation and change projects are *execution* processes. Individuals rarely have a natural competence in leading both types of activities. Strategy development projects require skills and competence in thought leadership and project management. Strategy implementation and change programs require skills and competence in change leadership and program management. Exhibits 2-4 and 2-5 compare and contrast these modes of leadership and management.

■ *Should we improve the governance and communications within and across the portfolio of strategy and change projects to ensure sufficient coordination and alignment?* Having committed project managers on strategy or change initiatives can be both a blessing and a curse. It takes a committed project manager to get projects done on time and within budget. But those same project managers can become overly protective and downright territorial with respect to their project. Unfortunately, the line between the project and the person begins to blur. The CEO will ask in passing how *your* project is coming along or how Elizabeth's project is doing. The success of the project becomes the success of the project leader. This creates behaviors, decisions, and actions that may be good for the project but not necessarily good for the corporation.

Thought Leadership	Change Leadership
• Creativity • Willingness to consider new ideas • Keeping oneself open to new possibilities • Dialogue rather than advocacy • Talking the talk is sufficient • Continuous vocal support of process tasks to project team • Thought oriented • Accountabilities are low • Drive to a decision around one idea • Business considerations are a central part of a decision	• Practicality • Willingness to try new ideas • Keeping others open to new possibilities • Advocacy rather than dialogue • Walking the talk is required • Continuous vocal support of implementation tasks to entire organization • Action oriented • Accountabilities are high • Drive to results by implementing the idea • Organizational considerations are a central part of actions

Exhibit 2-4 – Comparing characteristics of thought leadership to change leadership.

Project Management	Program Management
• Less visible and responsive to few • Smaller team working on tasks in series • Six-month or less schedule • Ability to adjust assumptions and boundaries • No requirement for broad organizational ownership • Produce commitment to an idea • Cost is managed by managing schedule • Quality of deliverable does not have immediate financial impact	• Highly visible and responsive to many • Large team with multiple sub-teams working on tasks in parallel • Over 1-year schedule • Boundaries are well-defined at the onset and are firm • Broad organizational ownership is a critical success factor • Deliver tangible, measurable results • Cost must be managed as well as schedule • Quality of deliverable has immediate financial impact

Exhibit 2-5 – Comparing characteristics of project management to program management.

The coordination and alignment among concomitant initiatives does not occur naturally. In fact, you can bet that concomitant initiatives will compete with each other—for resources and management attention—resulting in value-destroying behaviors, decisions, and actions. The CEO and COO should not become the traffic cops in the middle of these initiatives, but they often do. Playing this role may create a sense of power, but it is the wrong role. The CEO and COO should provide guidance, make critical decisions, resolve issues, and play an appropriate role in organizational alignment. To work the coordination, communications, performance tracking, and the overall organizational alignment of the portfolio of strategy and change initiatives, get a program manager.

■ *Is our current operations and organizational structure appropriate for the types of strategies we are considering?* If it is clear during the development of alternative corporate strategies that there must be significant change in operations or organizational structure, then those decisions should be injected into the work of creating the strategy. For example, if a significant cultural transformation is required to execute a strategy, then the desirable characteristics of this culture should be identified as part of the strategy. Cultural transformations can be momentous—it's wise to work on them as soon as possible.

Pinpointing and Measuring Value and Risk

A high-quality strategic decision, by our definition, requires clearly understanding the value and risk associated with the alternatives. Failing to pinpoint the sources of value and of risk and failing to measure them reduces decision making to a political process that can range from democratic and egalitarian to dictatorial and authoritarian. By pinpointing and measuring value and risk, we can explicitly say why one alternative is better than another. Moreover, by pinpointing and measuring value and risk we can often create hybrid alternatives that combine the best aspects of two or more separate alternatives to create a dominant alternative that offers maximum value while mitigating the largest sources of risk. These points are best illustrated with an example.

Case Study: The Trucking Division of Smithfield, Inc.

The trucking division of Smithfield, Inc., a component supplier to large truck manufacturers, was facing a flat market with no expected growth in the foreseeable future. The trucking division had been struggling for several years. Their component sales were unprofitable and the division was making money only on the service parts. The division's customers had been fighting to survive in the midst of an increasingly competitive market for trucks, and their precarious position made the company reluctant to raise prices. Smithfield's other divisions had higher volume, were growing, and consumed most of the company's attention and resources. Little investment had been made in the trucking division in recent years. The product line needed updating. Manufacturing costs for the trucking division were very high. Several executive team members believed that divestiture was the only real alternative, but Smithfield's CEO wanted to consider other alternative strategies.

Four strategies were constructed and analyzed:

1. *No Strings Attached:* The trucking division may not be profitable in the long-term; therefore, divest.

2. *Hit and Run:* The trucking division may not be profitable in the long term; therefore, we should exit. We can take care of our current customers by providing them with a source of supply—not at our expense—until the market replaces us.

3. *Focus and Fix:* Smithfield has a strong brand image and has maintained a reputation for excellence in the trucking division's markets. The company could rebuild the trucking division's position with new components and services, keeping the division viable and reducing costs.

4. *Go and Grow:* Smithfield could focus on recreating the marketplace and capturing some of the competitors' captive business. The trucking division would take an aggressive approach to the market and dominate it with new products and services, with aggressive cost reductions.

Using the net present value (NPV) of discounted cash flows as the metric to compare the four strategies, the "Go and Grow" strategy appeared to be the best path forward, as illustrated in Exhibit 2-6. By pinpointing and measuring the sources of value and risk, the executive team uncovered many insights, including why the "No Strings Attached" divestiture option was so unappealing. The results illustrated in Exhibit 2-7 make it clear that it would be better to divest later. The cost structure of the business

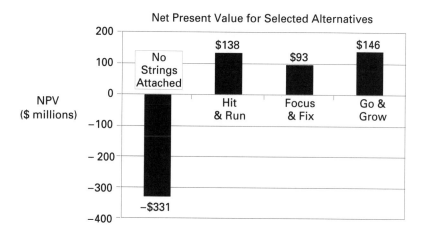

Exhibit 2-6 – Financial comparison of trucking division's alternative strategies.

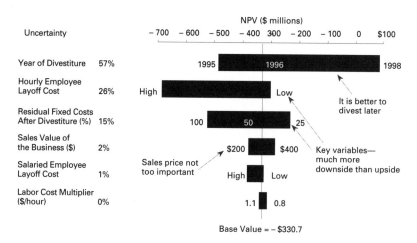

Exhibit 2-7 – Risk assessment of the no-strings-attached strategy.

makes divestiture unattractive because it would eliminate revenues but not costs. Even under the optimistic scenario, in which only 25 percent of the fixed overhead remained after the divestiture, the "No Strings Attached" alternative still had a negative NPV. The trucking division carried substantial allocated fixed costs, all of which would remain after the divestiture. On the other hand, delaying the divestiture maintained the revenue stream to offset fixed costs, thus improving the NPV. An optimistic sales price would not be enough to compensate for the costs that would remain. The executive team concluded that an immediate divestiture was not a viable alternative.

At this juncture, the executive team arrived at a dramatically different perspective about the business and established the following insights:

- Smithfield benefited financially by remaining in the trucking division's business longer. Immediate divestiture was not a good alternative.
- Cost reduction significantly improved NPV. The more aggressive the cost reduction, the greater the improvement in profitability.
- Price increases on both units and service parts also improved NPV, and prices should be increased in the future.
- The addition of a new set of components moderately improved cash flows.

The executive team developed two hybrid alternatives that were better than the original four:

1. A "short-term" hybrid strategy that focused on remaining in the business in the short term until customers replaced them with competitors. In the interim, the trucking division would increase prices and cut manufacturing investments. Additionally, the trucking division would maintain

current customer support and supply customers with current products.

2. A "long-term" hybrid strategy that focused on investing in the business for the long term. The trucking division would invest in aggressive cost reduction and raise prices to get the business on a sound financial footing. Additionally, the division would increase customer support significantly and develop a new series of components with a partner.

Both the "short-term" and the "long-term" hybrid strategies appeared to outperform the original best strategy of "Go and Grow," as illustrated in Exhibit 2-8. Moreover, when uncertainty was accounted for in the major risk drivers, the "long-term" strategy had a higher expected value and less down-side risk than the "short-term" strategy, as illustrated in Exhibit 2-9.

The executive team worried about the level of cost reductions projected in the "long-term" strategy. Many felt that while aggressive cost reductions would be valuable, the strategy was too ambitious to be managed effectively. The attention demanded by the

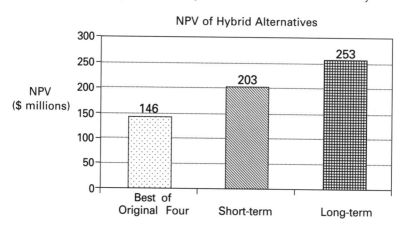

Exhibit 2-8 – Financial comparison of trucking division's hybrid strategies.

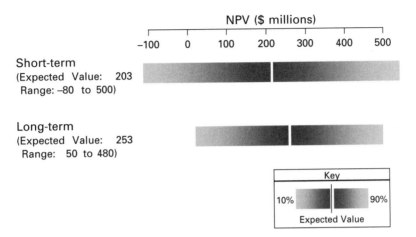

Exhibit 2-9 – Value and risk comparison of the hybrid alternatives.

other businesses of the components company reduced the amount of time and resources that could be dedicated to the trucking division. Several executives questioned whether the level of cost reductions was obtainable at all. The numbers were consistent with their experience elsewhere in the company, but several executives remained skeptical. If fewer cost reductions were realized, would they switch from "long-term" to "short-term"?

Some additional analysis revealed that the "long-term" strategy had the higher NPV even with only a 50 percent probability of achieving nominal cost reductions. Exhibit 2-10 illustrates the results of this analysis.

At this point, the CEO and his executive team decided to pursue the "long-term" strategy. Smithfield immediately pursued investing in aggressive cost reduction, raising prices, increasing customer support, and developing a new series of components with a partner. The executive team had learned why their initial inclination to divest was inappropriate. Taking the time to create and evaluate a hybrid added an additional 74 percent in NPV over and above the best of the original strategies they had be-

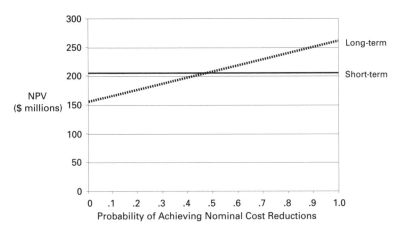

Exhibit 2-10 – Sensitivity of strategy selection with respect to cost reductions.

lieved to be compelling and attractive. As important as uncovering the best strategy by pinpointing and measuring the sources of value and risk, was the confidence that they had made a high-quality decision, which drove the commitment to implement.

CASE STUDY

Alpha Forest Products Looks Beyond the Conventional Wisdom

Strategy played a critical role in reversing the fortunes of AFP. Because capital equipment dominates the operating budget in the forest products industry, AFP had, from time immemorial, pursued a strategy that was operationally focused: Maximize the use of the capital equipment and keep production running 24/7/52.

In fact, the prevailing wisdom in the industry held that there were three ways to compete: operations, operations, and operations. For many forest products companies, the overriding goal was operational excellence, and it remains a central aim for many of them today.

AFP's senior executive team began to look beyond the conventional wisdom and its strategic corollary of seeking incremental operational improvements. The AFP team sought to understand the sources of value and risk in their business, and the relationships of that value and risk to the assets they owned, the operations they ran, and the outcomes they measured.

AFP's work on strategy produced concrete, quantitative evidence that their business was not one business, but many very different businesses. The value of their products and the risks those products faced in the marketplace varied greatly across the portfolio of products AFP could and did make. In fact, their strategy work showed that by changing focus from operational excellence and even operational dominance to a sense-and-respond, market-and-customer-focused strategy, they could vastly improve the financial performance of the business—and this at a time when they were in the bottom tier of performance in a down market with prices in the trough and worldwide capacity at its peak.

AFP's new strategy required that they understand the submarkets and micromarkets that constituted what had seemingly been a single, homogeneous commodity market. In order to understand the relative value of one product over another at a particular moment in time, AFP had to build a market-facing, market-based, market-intelligent organization. This was not a one-time fix; this was a new way of life.

Most importantly, the AFP team developed their strategy concurrently and systematically with the other interdependent elements of value: its asset portfolios, its organization and operations, and its financial structures and measures. The new strategy called for taking advantage of higher margin, value-added markets, which were currently being treated by competitors as traditional commodity markets. AFP's management understood that the bold, new strategy could succeed only if they optimized their asset portfolios, redesigned the organizational structure, and employed new financial measures.

But the breakthrough thinking had occurred. By explicitly understanding the key components of value and of risk within their business, they were able to see that the same people, using the same factories and employing the same machines, could make a different set of products where the value and profitability far exceeded that of their existing line. This entirely new view of their asset portfolios and performance was a significant breakthrough in and of itself. As a result, the company could perform far better in the marketplace than they would if they remained on their current course, carried along by momentum—or more accurately—inertia.

The keys to unlocking the value of asset portfolios is the topic of the next chapter.

Notes

1. *2001 Shareholder Value Survey* sponsored by Strategic Decisions Group.

Treating Asset Portfolios as Portfolios

CHAPTER THREE

"Time has a way of changing our
assets into liabilities."

—PETER F. DRUCKER, MANAGEMENT THINKER AND AUTHOR

In 1993, SmithKline Beecham was spending more than half a billion dollars annually on research and development. With an increasing number of R&D projects reaching the resource intensive late-stage development, R&D funding requirements were going through the roof. The patent on their blockbuster drug, Tagamet, was about to expire, exacerbating the growing tension between meeting near-term earnings requirements while supporting the necessary R&D to create their future sources of revenue. Of SmithKline Beecham's vast portfolio of R&D projects, which should receive increased investment? Which should have reduced budgets? Which should be terminated? What should be the overall R&D budget? And what is the risk versus return for that budget? All of these questions were critical and all of these questions represent portfolio management questions.

SmithKline Beecham went on to answer these questions and more by applying the tools and techniques discussed in this chapter, and they ultimately increased their return on investment, for the same level of investment, by 30 percent—an increase in return on investment of $2 billion. These same techniques, which have a variety of applications in corporations, will be addressed in this chapter.

CASE STUDY

Alpha Forest Products Refocuses on Its Asset Portfolios

With the new founded belief that the gateway to significantly improved financial performance was through shifting from operational excellence to a sense-and-respond, market- and customer-focused strategy with higher margin products, AFP put its many asset portfolios into play, including product, manufacturing facilities, and organizational capabilities. What products should be included in the product portfolio? What should be the overall product portfolio budget and allocation? How should product manufacturing be distributed across the portfolio of manufacturing facilities? What capabilities are required at each facility to capture the optimal product and manufacturing facility allocations?

What seemed like a complex, tangled web of decisions (both politically and analytically), with little hope for producing significant change and improvement over the current setting, proved to be one of the most fruitful endeavors in this time frame for AFP. Alpha Forest Products learned to manage their asset portfolios as portfolios.

Businesses as Asset Portfolios

The French novelist Marcel Proust said, "The secret is not in seeking new landscapes but in having new eyes." The lenses through which you view your business govern your ability to create effective strategies and make quality strategic decisions. By viewing your business from various portfolio perspectives you can uncover issues and challenges facing your business and generate creative, value-rich alternatives.

Every business can be viewed from many portfolio perspectives, such as portfolios of business units, markets, products and services, customers, intellectual property, R&D, facilities, competencies, functions, business processes, projects, capital investments, IT investments, people, and even risks. The goal is to maximize the expected return on investment in each of these portfolios. But sometimes a given portfolio must be suboptimized to get the most value for the corporation. Ultimately, maximizing shareholder value from the collection of portfolios requires the alignment of each of the portfolios with the corporation's business strategy, financial measures and structure, and organization and operations. Proust, though far from a CEO, had the fundamental insight in "having new eyes."

As Michael Allen of Strategic Decisions Group writes, "Even the best-managed portfolio companies can do better. . . . Most corporations can achieve striking increases in shareholder value through the strategic management of their portfolios of subsidiaries, business units, and product categories."[1] Allen states that to do so, they need to improve in:

- Creating real strategic alternatives
- Accurately estimating the value of those alternatives
- Understanding the risks involved in each alternative

Managing asset portfolios requires answering several fundamental questions, including:

- What is the appropriate level of funding for the overall portfolio of opportunities?
- Are there areas in the portfolio where funding should be increased? If yes, by how much?
- Are there areas in the portfolio where funding should be reduced? If yes, by how much?
- Are there new areas of investment that should be added and are there areas that should be eliminated?
- How does investment A compare to investment B with respect to required investment and expected benefit?
- Which assets should be outsourced and which should be insourced?
- What assets should be acquired, what assets should be divested, and which should be licensed?
- Where is the current investment plan in relation to the efficient frontier of investments for the portfolio?
- What can be done to push the portfolio performance beyond the current efficient frontier?

To understand how to apply portfolio theory and portfolio management to these various forms of asset portfolios, let's start with the foundation of the theory, the *efficient frontier,* briefly introduced in Chapter 1.

The Efficient Frontier and Efficient Portfolios

The notion of an efficient frontier can greatly improve decision making in portfolio management. Most readers are familiar with the concept from the context of their own financial investments. As a financial investor, you have available to you low-risk assets such as treasury bills (T-bills) and bank certificate of deposits (CDs), various corporate stocks and bonds, and high-risk emerging market opportunities. You can create many different investment portfolios for a given level of investment by picking investment opportunities from across this risk-and-return spectrum. Each portfolio of investments selected has a risk-and-return profile that can be determined through financial analysis.

Exhibit 3-1 shows seven such portfolios that use risk versus return as the trade-off. Investors must choose the portfolio that has the right risk and return trade-off, depending on their aversion to risk and need for return. Only four of these seven portfolios should be considered for investment—portfolios A, B, D, and G—since they yield the greatest expected return for a given level of risk. These portfolios lie along the *efficient frontier.*

The concept of an efficient frontier can be applied in a num-

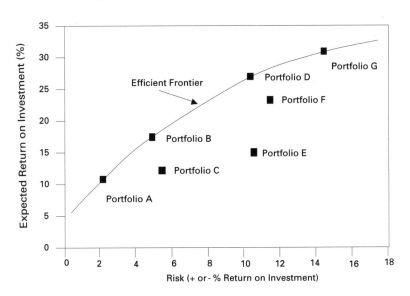

Exhibit 3-1 – Risk-versus-return efficient frontier.

ber of ways. In essence, an *efficient frontier* is a curve on a graph representing the relationship between return (or a measure of benefit) and risk (or a measure of cost) for a set of portfolios. For a portfolio to be on the efficient frontier, the portfolio must maximize return (or benefit) for a given level of risk (or cost). As shown in Exhibit 3-1, Portfolio A has a low expected return but also has low risk. Portfolio G has a high expected return but has relatively high risk. All other portfolios lie between these two ends of the risk-versus-return spectrum. Portfolio E has the same level of risk as Portfolio D, but Portfolio D has a much higher expected return. Thus Portfolio D should always be chosen over Portfolio E. Portfolios C, E, and F are all inferior portfolios and are deemed *inefficient*. As an investor considering these opportunities, you would choose Portfolio A, B, D, or G, depending on your personal trade-off between need for return and aversion to risk. An *efficient portfolio* is one that offers the greatest expected return (or benefit) for a given level of risk (or cost).[2]

The same notion of an efficient frontier applies to the many asset portfolios within a business. CEOs make investments and manage the portfolio of business units; business unit executives make investments and manage portfolios of products and projects; R&D managers make investments and manage the portfolio of R&D projects; COOs make investments and manage the portfolio of business processes and facilities; CIOs make investments and manage the portfolio of IT projects; contract program and project managers make investments and manage the risks of systems development and implementation. The good news is that the same concept and approaches apply to each of these classes of portfolios. What differs in these portfolios are the trade-offs to be made and the means of displaying the results in order to highlight the key insights of the analyses in support of budget setting and allocation.

Applying the Concept of Efficient Frontier to Asset Portfolios

For a concrete example of how to construct an efficient frontier, consider a portfolio of three capital projects: A, B, and C. The key to getting the most from any portfolio lies in the quality of the alternatives considered. For each of the three capital projects four alternatives were developed and analyzed, including the current capital project plan, an "aggressive" plan, a cutback in funding plan, and no funding. For each project and for each level of investment, the net present value (NPV) of discounted cash flows was computed. The results of the financial analyses are presented in Exhibit 3-2. Note that the no-funding alternatives have been treated in a simplified manner by assuming that no investment implied a zero NPV of cash flows. If any of these projects had been on-going, there would have been cost of termination that could easily result in negative NPV of cash flow.

There are sixty-four possible portfolios from this table of investment and return, which are graphed in Exhibit 3-3. For any given investment level there is a portfolio that will maximize the

	Project A		Project B		Project C	
Plan	NPV Capital (M$)	NPV CF (M$)	NPV Capital (M$)	NPV CF (M$)	NPV Capital (M$)	NPV CF (M$)
Aggressive	5	35	8	50	3	5
Current	2	10	5	40	2	3
Cut Back	1	3	1	5	1	1
No Funding	0	0	0	0	0	0

Exhibit 3-2 – Investment and return for of four alternatives for three capital projects.

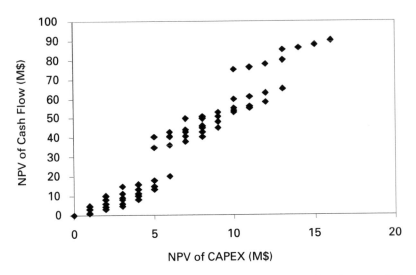

Exhibit 3-3 – Plot of investment and return possibilities for three capital projects.

return on investment. For example, for a capital investment of $10 million the portfolio with highest return includes aggressive pursuit of project A at a $5 million capital investment, proceed with the current plan of a $5 million investment in project B, and terminate project C. Incidentally, the current plan in this case is on the efficient frontier. In many cases, the first insight from these analyses is how far current plans are from the efficient frontier. Applying the concept well requires deciding what trade-offs to use for each of the classes of portfolios.

Portfolio of Businesses

The trade-off most corporate executives face on a daily basis is that of shareholder value versus short-term earnings. Although most executives today would say that shareholder value matters most, the near-term performance of the corporation's stock price is always on their minds. With stock analysts and investors alike waiting for quarterly earnings reports to determine their next investment move, executives know they must strike a balance between the pursuit of shareholder value and short-term earnings. This is a significant challenge since major gains in shareholder value are rarely attributable to activities that produce short-term gains. For example, pharmaceutical companies plough big dollars into R&D activities that won't generate revenues for years. Oil and gas investments can have even longer time horizons to profits.

Consider the corporate strategy of a large electronics corporation with four business units: consumer products, semiconductors, software and services, and lighting. Each of these four business units was asked to create three to four significantly different yet compelling strategies for their business unit. They were also asked to provide two measures for each business unit strategy—the expected current earnings per share, and the shareholder value created by each strategy as measured in terms of NPV of discounted cash flow per share. If each of the four business units created four separate strategies, the number of possible combinations is four to the fourth power, or 256 different business unit strategy portfolios! With no attempt to align or coordinate the strategies across the four business units, the majority of these portfolios would fall on the interior of the corporation's efficient frontier, as depicted in Exhibit 3-4.

The role of the CEO and other corporate executives is to align the business unit strategies to get more of what the shareholders want, and that is both long-term value as measured in shareholder value and current quarter or near-quarter earnings per share. When business unit strategies are aligned along some corporate vision, the values of the corporate portfolio of business unit strategies begin to approach the efficient frontier. As we will see, going beyond the efficient frontier requires aligning asset portfolios with corporate strategy, the corporate financial measures and structure, and the organization and operations of the corporation.

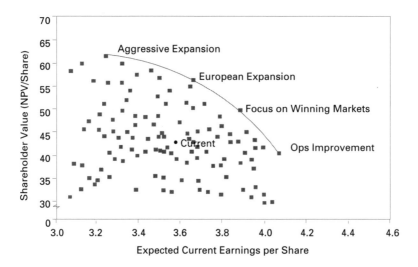

Exhibit 3-4 – Shareholder value versus expected current earnings efficient frontier.

The typical placement of corporate level strategies cascaded down into business units is illustrated in Exhibit 3-4. Cost-cutting and operational improvement strategies tend to yield near-term results at the expense of long-term value creation. Consequently, they fall into the southeast area of the efficient frontier. Aggressive-growth corporate strategies require heavy investment and are consequently hard on current earnings per share while promising maximum long-term value creation.

Using the concept of efficient frontier as a benchmark for gauging levels of corporate financial performance, Michael Allen details a method for creating and evaluating corporate level strategies for corporations consisting of multi- and varied business units.[3] To do this well, you must base the strategic planning process on assessing alternatives, quantitatively measure value and risk, and use a financial measurement system that correctly accounts for the relationship and trade-offs in value and risk.

Portfolio of Projects

Classes of project-based portfolios include capital-intensive projects, research and development projects, product development, process improvements, information technology investments, and pursuit of contract revenue. Many of these classes of portfolios have a set of investments that must be pursued such as maintenance of heavy equipment in a portfolio of capital projects or maintenance of IT systems in a portfolio of IT investments. "Must-have" investments, which should be excluded from the analysis, should be kept to a minimum. Most organizations tend to fill-up the "must-have" investments with pet projects, which minimizes the discretionary value-building investments and ultimately dampens the potential return on the portfolio of investment opportunities. You should frequently and regularly scrutinize "must-have" investments to ensure that they really represent investments that should be continued or at least maintained at the planned level of investment.

To understand the evaluation and management of a project portfolio, consider businesses in industries such as aerospace, services, engineering and construction, and manufacturing. Their revenue comes from contracts won in a competitive market. A defense contractor, for example, makes primarily three forms of investment in the pursuit of new contracts: research and development (R&D), selling expense, and bid and proposal expense, collectively referred to here as new business investment (NBI). Capital investment is often small, because it is typically built into the contract being pursued, so it will not be considered in this example.

A defense contractor must answer the fundamental portfolio questions, listed at the beginning of this chapter, as well as the following:

- Should we allocate more NBI in domestic programs and cut back our international investments?

- With respect to required investment and expected return, how does investment in avionics compare to investments in battlefield electronics?
- What are the dependencies in capturing these contracts and to what degree are they dependent?

Understanding the impacts of contract dependencies and having multiple ways to segment the portfolio of contract opportunities is critical for revealing how best to place the corporation's new business investment bets.

To evaluate the portfolio of contract opportunities for risk and return, three types of information must be collected for each opportunity:

1. *NBI Requirements:* R&D investment, selling expense, and bid-and-proposal expense for the current year and future year requirements. (Capital should be included if it is a required form of investment.)

2. *Probability of Capture:* calculated as the probability of the contract being awarded multiplied by the probability of winning the contract.

3. *Operating Earnings:* annual operating earnings resulting from the NBI. (We use operating earnings, as opposed to cash flow, because organizations routinely document operating earnings for financial forecasting. If capital charges were included, then we would use cash flow for proper accounting of capital.)

If winning or losing a specific contract impacts the probability of winning a subsequent contract, than the two contracts are dependent. For correct accounting of contract dependence, contracts that are dependent should be bundled. Exhibit 3-5 illustrates a portfolio investment risk-versus-return grid that provides a perspective on the spread of risk versus return for the complete portfolio of contract opportunities.

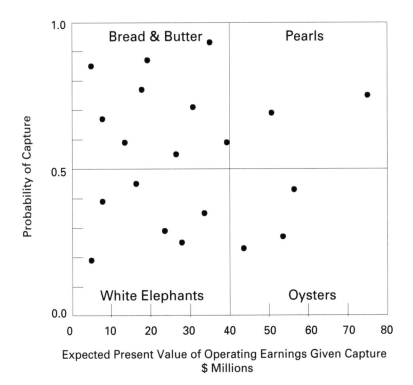

Exhibit 3-5 – Portfolio investment risk versus return grid for a defense contractor.

Matheson and Matheson[4] detail the concept of an R&D grid that is analogous to the grid in Exhibit 3-5 for portfolios consisting of R&D projects. Each point on the grid represents a contract or bundle of dependent contracts. The vertical axis represents the probability of capturing the contract and the horizontal axis represents the expected present value of the operating earnings associated with the contract, assuming the contract is captured. The grid splits the contract opportunities into four quadrants:

Bread and Butter: These are contract opportunities that have a high probability of capture but have relatively low value. They are needed to maintain short-term financial performance and cash flow. Much of the investment in this quadrant goes toward building on existing products, markets, and contracts.

Pearls: This quadrant contains contract opportunities that have a relatively high probability of capture and high value. They are needed to establish long-term growth and typically consist of revolutionary advances of proven technologies or large-scale applications of proven technologies. The large-scale applications can be in the opening of new markets, such as foreign military sales, or the roll-out of a technology into broad application, such as using an aircraft's display system in automobiles. As you would suspect, the problem with most portfolios upon initial evaluation is their dearth of pearls.

Oysters: These are the contracts with low probability of capture but high value. The question here is what can be done to make these oysters into pearls. Some of these opportunities may simply be starved for resources. Others may have a low probability of capture due to the extremely competitive nature of the opportunity. A healthy portfolio needs to have some of these bets. By constructing this grid, you can get the portfolio perspective required to adjust the portfolio for the right spread of risk and return desired by the shareholders.

White Elephants:[5] These are the contracts with low probability of capture and low value. Unfortunately, initial evaluations of contract portfolios and, in fact, most classes of portfolios typically reveal too many white elephants. Why? Gold mines of business opportunities eventually run dry. Product lines age. Markets change. Competitors reposition themselves and their products. Before management realizes it, they are making investments that made sense one, two, or even three years before; however, these investments don't make sense today, given the opportunities going forward. Many individuals in the organization will defend the white elephant opportunities, offering many reasons why they should be kept in the budget. "We have been investing in this for the past three years, we will lose all our investment if we give up now."

You recognize this as an issue of sunk cost. "This is a pet project of our most important customer." "We need to pursue this to keep our customer satisfied." "We need this activity to maintain our R&D staff; what else are they going to work on?" While some of these concerns may be valid, they should be considered in the context of getting the most out of the investments in the portfolio; that is, the concerns need to be aligned with the strategic goals and objectives of the corporate strategy and the goals and objectives of the portfolio. The grid helps uncover these ubiquitous issues and errors in judgment.

Once this portfolio perspective has been established, several actions should be taken in managing the portfolio of opportunities:

1. Capture the pearls.
2. Eliminate or reposition the white elephants.
3. Based on the corporation's aversion to risk and cash flow requirements, balance the investments across the bread and butter opportunities with the oysters to ensure alignment in these investments with the corporation's strategy, the corporation's financial measures and structure, and the corporation's organization and operations. (We will address this in a subsequent section of this chapter.)

Balancing the investments correctly requires one more perspective on the portfolio of opportunities: the *investment productivity curve*. A productivity measure indicates the "bang for the buck" on an investment. In the case of the defense contractor, an NBI productivity measure equals the probability of capture multiplied by the expected present value of operating earnings divided by the present value of the NBI requirements (that is, the investment). If we put the investments in descending order by their NBI productivity measure and plot them by their cumulative impact on return and cumulative impact on investment, we get a graph like that depicted in Exhibit 3-6. The curve measures cumulative expected return as a function of cumulative expected investment. Beginning from the origin, the first point on the graph is the investment in the contract with the highest NBI productivity measure. Each subsequent point on the graph represents the incremental investment and incremental return for the next highest productive investment.

What is immediately obvious in Exhibit 3-6 is the diminishing returns associated with the new business investments as currently planned. We typically see the Pareto 80/20 rule in such evaluations, which is that 80 percent of the value is associated with 20 percent of the new business investment. The last few projects on the tail of the curve will include many of the white elephant projects, yielding returns that teeter around $1 of expected return for $1 of investment—not a very appealing return on investment.

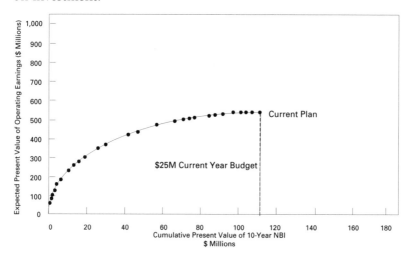

Exhibit 3-6 – New business investment productivity curve for a defense contractor.

Understanding the impact of changes in strategy and NBI funding on the productivity of each investment provides sufficient information to optimize the value of the portfolio and move it onto the efficient frontier of investments. Exhibit 3-7 illustrates what information must be collected to optimize the NBI investments for productivity. By selecting the investment strategy with the highest expected productivity for each contract opportunity, you can re-create a second investment productivity curve that optimizes the return on investment. Exhibit 3-8 illustrates the impact of reallocating investments based on maximum bang for the buck for each opportunity. Evident in Exhibit 3-8 is the significant increase in return for the same budget level.

In this case, based upon this analysis, there was a 35 percent increase in expected return resulting from the reallocation of new business investment. This maximum bang for the buck productivity curve represents an efficient portfolio of contract investments and thus is on the efficient frontier of the contract investment opportunities. In our experience, the improvement in expected return for asset portfolios of all forms typically falls between 30 percent and 40 percent when applying these approaches. Sharpe and Keelin[6] reported a $2 billion increase in expected return for the R&D portfolio at SmithKline Beecham by

NBI Level	Probability of Capture	NBI ($K)	Earnings ($M)	Expected Productivity
Increased	0.70	400	2.7	4.7
Current	0.55	250	2.8	6.2
Reduced	0.20	100	1.5	3.0
Minimal	0.00	10	0.0	0.0

Exhibit 3-7 – Four investment strategies and their respective measures of productivity for a contract opportunity.

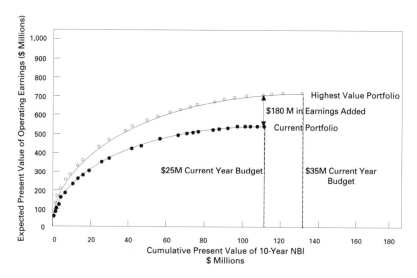

Exhibit 3-8 – Comparison of financial performance of an optimal allocation of contract investments to the current plan.

using these approaches, which translates into a 30 percent increase in expected return.

In some cases, the projects in a portfolio of potential projects could number well over a hundred and sometimes in the several hundreds. In these cases, it is impractical to create multiple investment strategies for each investment. You should select the projects that merit a deeper understanding of investment strategy and then create multiple investment strategies for these select projects, as illustrated in Exhibit 3-7. All remaining projects should then be treated as investments with one investment strategy, either the current plan or a revised "best and final" plan.

Using these same approaches, it is helpful to segment the investment portfolio and understand and contrast the performance of various portfolio segments. Instead of each point on the graphs representing individual contracts or groups of dependent contracts, each point would represent a segment of investments.

For the defense contractor there are several segmentations that are useful and insightful, including segmenting by product line, geography, sole source contracts versus competitive contracts, current plan projects versus potential plan projects, technology, new business versus follow-on, or cross-divisional projects versus single division projects.

Exhibit 3-9 summarizes the defense contractor's critical performance measures for the NBI portfolio as segmented by prod-

	Entire Portfolio	Product-line				
		A	B	C	D	E
Throughput	65%	59%	62%	61%	93%	33%
Potential Productivity	7.7	6.5	14.5	5.5	18.8	7.0
Expected Productivity	5.0	3.8	8.9	3.4	17.6	2.3
Percentage of Current Year Budget	100%	3.8%	6.8%	3.0%	7.9%	4.1%
Percentage of 10-Year Budget	100%	6.3%	10.9%	3.0%	10.4%	4.4%

$$\text{Potential Productivity} = \frac{\Sigma\, E}{\Sigma\, C} = \text{"The most we could get"}$$

$$\text{Expected Productivity} = \frac{\Sigma\,(P*E)}{\Sigma\, C} = \text{"What we expect to get"}$$

$$\text{Throughput} = \frac{\text{Exp. Prod.}}{\text{Pot. Prod.}} = \frac{\text{"Fraction of potential we}}{\text{expect to get"}}$$

P = Probability of capture
E = Present value of operating earnings
C = Present value of the new business investments including: R&D, selling expense, and bid and proposal expense

Exhibit 3-9 – Example of critical portfolio performance measures for a product-line segmentation of a new business investment portfolio.

uct line. This table introduces a couple of additional portfolio measures that help uncover the value creation potential of these investments:

The **potential productivity** of a collection of investments equals the sum of the present values of the potential operating earnings divided by the sum of the present values of the costs to capture. This ratio represents the ceiling or the maximum productivity possible. It represents the productivity of the collection of investments, assuming that the defense contractor captures every contract pursued. In simple terms, this represents the most the defense contractor can get for the investment.

The **expected productivity** of a collection of investments equals the sum of the present values of the expected operating earnings divided by the sum of the present values of the costs to capture. In simple terms, this represents what the defense contractor actually expects to get for the investments.

The **throughput** of a collection of investments represents the fraction of potential return that the defense contractor expects to get and is defined as the expected productivity divided by the potential productivity.

Consequently, when scanning these measures, look for such things as low throughput values, which suggests that you're not getting your share of return for a collection of investments. For example, in Exhibit 3-9 the question is why product line E has a throughput of only 33 percent. You need to investigate and determine what can be done to reposition and improve this investment or determine whether you should stop investing in this product line. Of course, you are also trying to identify which segments of the overall portfolio provide the best returns and which provide the worst. By performing several different segment analyses you can uncover the hidden story of value potential in the portfolio.

Armed with those insights, the defense contractor could answer the many questions that arise in portfolio management:

- What is the appropriate level of funding for the overall portfolio of opportunities?
    - Referring back to Exhibit 3-8, a current budget of between $30 million to $35 million will maximize the value of the portfolio and will fund business areas with expected returns of 4 to 1.
- Are there areas in the portfolio where funding should be increased? If yes, by how much?
    - Unmanned Automated Vehicles (UAVs) is an oyster that could use an additional $3 million in R&D to speed up the time to market. We also need an additional $1 million in marketing for the Asia/Pacific market.
- Are there areas in the portfolio where funding should be reduced? If yes, by how much?
    - Air traffic control systems should be reduced in funding to a minimal level until we determine where Congress is going with the budgets. We also should reduce marketing expenses in Western Europe.
- Are there new areas of investment that should be added and are there areas that should be eliminated?
    - Undersea weapons and toll road development are the two businesses with the lowest productivity scores; consider both for either repositioning or divestment.
- With respect to required investment and expected return, how does investment in avionics compare to investments in battlefield electronics?
    - Avionics and battlefield electronics will require $8 million and $3 million new business investment respectively; however, the avionics business expects a return of 8 to 1 as compared to 4.5 to 1 for battlefield electronics. The portfolio return is 5 to 1.

■ What are the dependencies in capturing these contracts and to what degree are they dependent?

▶ Capturing the land mine detection and de-mining markets is highly dependent on winning one of the two next major contracts. If we don't have at least a probability of 70 percent of winning one of the contracts, we should create an exit strategy.

We have taken a deep dive into how to apply portfolio management techniques to portfolios of contract revenue. The same approach applies to all of the other forms of project portfolios, including capital-intensive projects, research and development projects, product development, process improvements, and information technology investments. Exhibit 3-10 lists some suggested measures to use in applying these approaches.

Of the six types of project portfolios, process improvement and IT investments require the most ingenuity in evaluation because they create value in many dimensions. Each of these two types of project portfolios create value in at least six ways:

1. Annual cost savings derived from decreases in excess inventory
2. Annual improvements in productivity
3. Annual operations and maintenance savings
4. Annual deferred capital
5. Annual avoided liability or failure
6. Incremental increase in customers/sales due to perceived improvements

Consequently, when evaluating the benefits of these investments in terms of either operating earnings or cash flow, these six contributing factors, at the least, must be considered in the analysis.

Project Portfolio Type	Risk Versus Return Grid		Investment Productivity Curve	
	Horizontal Axis	Vertical Axis	Horizontal Axis	Vertical Axis
Capital Intensive Projects	Expected NPV of DCF	Probability of First Hurdle Success	Cumulative PV of Expected CAPEX	Cumulative Expected NPV of DCF
R&D Projects	Expected NPV of Commercial Value Given Technical Success	Probability of Technical Success	Cumulative PV of Expected Cost	Cumulative Expected NPV of DCF
Product Development Projects	Expected NPV of Commercial Value Given Technical Success	Probability of Technical Success	Cumulative PV of Expected Cost	Cumulative Expected NPV of DCF
Process Improvement Projects	Expected PV of Operating Earnings Given Capture	Probability of Achieving Target Improvements	Cumulative PV of Expected Cost	Cumulative Present Value of Operating Earnings
IT Projects	Expected PV of Operating Earnings Given Successful Completion	Probability of Successful Completion	Cumulative PV of Expected Cost	Cumulative Present Value of Operating Earnings
Contract Pursuits	Expected PV of Operating Earnings Given Capture	Probability of Capture	Cumulative PV of Expected New Business Investment	Cumulative Present Value of Operating Earnings

Exhibit 3-10 – Portfolio analysis measures for various classes of project portfolios.

Portfolio of Physical Assets

Portfolios of physical assets are similar in treatment to portfolios of projects, and there is some obvious overlap. However, in many cases another important portfolio of assets intersects with the portfolio of physical assets: the portfolio of people and competencies. In merger and acquisition strategies, significant perceived value is often tied to the closing of a facility. It looks good on paper, until you realize that the facility targeted for closing contains a significant set of core competencies in the resident employees. The strategists assume that the key people at the facility would be willing to uproot their families and move to the city where the facilities will be consolidated.

When that assumption proves to be false, two things inevitably happen. First, the facility targeted for closure remains open, sometimes indefinitely. Second, the most capable and valuable employees see the "writing on the wall" and begin searching for new employment. The painful result for the corporation is all too often a "black sheep" location or facility, which has lost its most valuable talent and limps along with low employee morale and low productivity. When facilities include significant heavy equipment like paper-making machines in a paper mill or refinery equipment in an oil refinery, you often must consider the human impact when modifying the portfolio since humans are needed to run the equipment. You can apply the portfolio techniques discussed here to equipment and facilities, but you must do it while also considering the impacts on the employees.

Portfolio of People and Competencies

Gary Hamel and C.K. Prahalad[7] introduced the notion of core competencies and the importance of identifying, understanding, growing, and protecting corporate core competencies in business. People and competencies represent the human capital in a corporation's value proposition. While human capital is universally recognized as a key asset, less is understood about how to value it. As with all asset portfolios, you must be able to measure the value and risk of the elements of the portfolio in order to manage it for optimal return on investment and position it on the efficient frontier.

How many times have you heard CEOs say something like "the value of our business is in our committed employees," or, "it's our employees that really make us stand out from our competitors." These plaudits usually draw snickers in the corporation's cafeterias, where employees cynically counter with "then why did you just reduce our pension plan and freeze raises this year?" For the most part, however, executives do understand that employees are fundamental to corporate value creation, but they struggle with how to measure it, and consequently with how to manage it from the perspective of maximizing return on investment across a portfolio of such assets.

Investment in human capital is very similar to other capital investments. There are four stages in the life cycle of an employee: acquisition, competency build-up, productivity and ongoing development, and attrition. Each stage has measurable costs and benefits. Each job title has typical or average lengths of stages, expected costs, and expected benefits. Does this sound like a capital project? It should because it is.

Every organization in a corporation has a portfolio of human capital projects, and they have names like John and Jennifer. When making investments in individuals and jobs, Human Resources staffs have alternatives to trade off, such as increasing investment to acquire more talented individuals, or providing excellent training to stimulate higher productivity and lengthen employment tenure. Too often, investment in human capital is a knee-jerk reaction to the current cash flow of a business. But if people and competencies are core asset portfolios, then they should be treated as such with a balanced short-term and long-term perspective.

To truly treat the portfolio of people and competencies as a portfolio with measurable financial return, we must map employee productivity, however measured, into a primary financial measure, such as net present value of discounted cash flows, economic value added (EVA), or cash flow return on investment (CFROI). This topic, however, lies well beyond the scope of this book.[8] In short, value-driver mapping or financial relationship mapping can be approached from a business process perspective or an activity-based perspective to uncover the relationships between work and financial return. The breakthrough is to consider people and competencies as asset portfolios that have both short-term and long-term returns and risks.

The fundamental questions and decisions about people and competency assets include:

- How to create incentives to maximize the return on the portfolio?
- Whether to outsource or insource specific competencies?
- How to acquire people and competencies while balancing a short-term acquisition perspective with an employee life-cycle perspective (costs and benefits)?
- How to understand the short-term and long-term consequences of training and development?

The competency and responsibility for managing the people and competency portfolio of assets should be with the Human Resources function of the organization.

Portfolio of Risks

Projects, business units, markets, strategies, mergers, organizations, governments, relationships, and people all have at least one thing in common. They all have associated risks. When these are considered as investment opportunities under the banner of risk management, we immediately realize that risk too can be viewed from the perspective of a portfolio.

Project risk management has grown in popularity over the past two decades. Requests for Proposals (RFPs) on contract projects for large-scale developments such as highways, communication systems, and software development often require risk management as part of the project contract and deliverables. Risk management processes imbedded in these projects will have steps including risk identification and assessment, risk mitigation strategy development and selection, risk mitigation, risk tracking, and risk closure. Intrinsic to risk management is the challenge of making the best risk mitigation investments from a limited budget in the face of a multitude of risks. It is, once again, a portfolio problem.

Collecting a risk inventory requires both a top-down and bottom-up approach, whether for a single project or for an entire corporation. Risk managing strategies should be constructed top-down to ensure a portfolio perspective and, ultimately, to achieve the maximum return on investment for the portfolio. For any specific risk item or family of risk items, you should consider four prospective strategies:

Risk Reduction: This risk management strategy is also referred to as risk abatement or risk mitigation. It is the approach most often used as a risk management plan. To reduce the risk associated with a risk item, you can reduce the probability of the risk occurring, reduce or eliminate the consequence of the risk item if it occurs, or both. Risk reduction can only be implemented when some aspect of the risk item is controllable.

Risk Transference: This approach is analogous to insurance. It requires a third party (perhaps the next level up in the organization or a subcontractor) to share the consequence if the risk occurs. Thus the emphasis is on reducing the consequence of the risk. Risk transference is often appropriate when the consequence of the risk is great but the probability of occurrence is low.

Resource Reservation: A set of resources is held in reserve or in a contingency fund to be used to absorb the impact of the risk should it occur.

Risk Assumption: Actually, this is not a risk management strategy at all. This approach is used when the risk item is assessed and it is decided that the corporation or program will do (or can do) nothing to mitigate the risk. The corporation or program assumes responsibility for the risk and its potential impact.

Risk management productivity curves can be constructed to ensure that investments in risk management are efficient and returning the maximum bang for the buck.

Focusing on the Core Components of Asset Portfolios and Filling the Portfolio Gaps

Every asset portfolio has core components that are critical to the performance of the portfolio and should be managed as such. What is considered a core component of an asset portfolio changes over time, so you should regularly determine what is core and what will be core in the future.

The difference between the current asset portfolio and a targeted, future portfolio is called the *portfolio gap*. It has two dimensions: one, the difference between the current performance of the portfolio and the targeted portfolio of a future state, and two, the difference between the contents of the portfolio today and the contents of the targeted portfolio in a future state. Considering the core components of an asset portfolio requires a continuous view of the current state and a targeted, future state so that you can determine the best way to transition from the current state to the future state. To get asset portfolios to change coherently and optimally over time you must align the performance and contents of the portfolios with the corporate strategy, the corporate financial measures and structure, and the organization and operations.

As utilities were scrapping, decommissioning, and selling

aging nuclear energy plants in the 1990s in order to rid their power-generation portfolios of this type of power, Entergy was busy reinforcing their competency in maintaining and running nuclear facilities. In direct contrast to the vast majority of utilities in the country, Entergy intended to buy nuclear plants and run them more efficiently than the current owners did—and at a profit. Entergy regarded maintaining and running nuclear power generation facilities as a core component of their current and future competency portfolio, and nuclear power generation plants were a growing core component of their physical asset portfolio.

A component of an asset portfolio is core if it is critical for the success of the corporate strategy and the corporation's *future* business model, or if the component is critical for retaining committed core staff with core competencies. Equally important, the core component does not have to be currently producing a significant share of the corporation's profitability. An asset performing at this level may be worth more to someone else, which suggests divestiture as a potential optimal asset strategy rather than nurturing the asset within the corporation. The key is to remain focused on the future destination of the corporate strategy and to continually work toward filling the portfolio gap.

Identifying the core components of an asset portfolio and specifying the portfolio gap helps keep the priority of investments in an asset portfolio focused on the "care and feeding" of these core components. Moreover, making explicit across an executive team what is considered the core components of the asset portfolios spares the executive team some of the confusion and misunderstandings that arise in accomplishing strategic changes. In some cases, explicitly identifying core components and their importance will help minimize some of the value-destroying behaviors that arise when an asset portfolio and the individual responsible for it become indistinguishable, sharing the same reputations and performance attribution.

Who Should Manage Asset Portfolios?

Relentless focus on asset portfolios from the perspective of core components and portfolio gaps happens only when a single individual is responsible and accountable for the performance of an asset portfolio. But who should that be?

Think of each asset portfolio in your organization as a mutual fund portfolio. Mutual fund portfolios have portfolio managers. Portfolio managers of mutual funds are ultimately responsible and accountable for the overall financial performance of their funds. These responsibilities include:

- Constructing the portfolio and changing its holdings over time
- Tracking the performance of the portfolio and ensuring that it meets the performance targets
- Managing the risk of the portfolio and ensuring that the degree of risk remains within the limits of the design of the portfolio

Using the mutual fund portfolio manager as the model, each asset portfolio in a corporation should have a portfolio manager. Many of the asset portfolios naturally do. Exhibit 3-11 suggests potential candidates for managing the various asset portfolios.

Asset Portfolios Must Be Aligned with Strategy

In Chapter 2 we discussed the view of asset portfolios that should be taken during the course of corporate strategy development, that is, the appropriate perspective of strategy development to asset portfolios. The reciprocal perspective is that of the asset portfolio manager to strategy development.

Although applying the concept of the efficient frontier to the business's asset portfolios is a must for maximizing return on investment within a given portfolio, it does not ensure maximum

Asset Portfolio	Potential Portfolio Manager
Business Units	CEO, COO, V.P. of Business Development
Capital Projects	COO at Corp. or Business Unit Level
Research and Development	V.P. of R&D
Product Development	COO at Corp. or BU Level, V.P. of Bus. Dev.
Process Improvement	COO at Corp. or BU Level, V.P. of Operations
Information Technology	Chief Information Officer (CIO)
Revenue Contracts	CFO at Corp. or BU Level, V.P. of Bus. Dev.
Equipment	V.P. of Operations and Maintenance
Facilities	COO at Corp. or BU Level, V.P. of O&M
People and Competencies	V.P. of Human Resources
Risks	CFO, V.P. of Risk Management

Exhibit 3-11 – Potential asset portfolio managers for a corporation's various asset portfolios.

shareholder value for the business. You must go beyond individual portfolio efficiencies. The portfolio of assets must be aligned and balanced with the pursuit of the future business model, with the current capital structure of the business and the pursuit of a desired capital structure, and with the orchestrated changes going on throughout the organization in the pursuit of the future business model.

Using the concept of efficient frontiers provides two key benefits. First, it identifies suboptimal portfolios where the performance should be considered as part of the strategy. Second, it highlights the various high performance portfolio options, which become a menu from which to select when you align the various portfolios to a business strategy or business model. By using a primary financial measure, such as the net present value of cash flows, as the financial measure in *all* portfolio analyses, trade-offs across portfolios can be made when capital budget pressures arise, as they always do.

When you consider asset portfolios in light of decisions and actions in the corporation's business strategy or model, its financial measures and structure, and its organization and operations, you can expand the efficient frontier of any one portfolio. Remember, the key to high-value portfolios and their placement of the efficient frontier is in the quality of the alternatives. When a pharmaceutical company considers a merger or acquisition to fill a gap in its product pipeline, the entire R&D efficient frontier shifts outward to reflect the additional alternatives and opportunities in the merged R&D portfolio.

In fact, a good acid test for a merger or acquisition is whether it expands the efficient frontier of the business. If it doesn't, then there is no value to be gained from it. An acquisition is one strategic alternative for a corporation (or portfolio of business units). So the acquisition target must be evaluated in the same way as internally focused strategies. If the acquisition falls beneath the corporation's efficient frontier, then the acquisition would actually reduce shareholder value.

When changing an asset portfolio you should consider these questions:

■ *What are the core components of the asset portfolio that are required to support the corporate strategy and future business model?* What is currently considered a core component may not be a core component in the future business model. For Entergy, a core component of their people and competencies portfolio was nuclear energy plant operations and maintenance.

■ *What is the current portfolio gap?* Remember, the portfolio gap is measured in terms of both performance and content. The performance of asset portfolios should be tracked over time for the purpose of benchmarking. This tracking should be extended to include external companies and organizations, when their performance measures are available.

■ *What are the strategic decisions regarding the asset portfolio, given the corporate strategy and future business model?* While the decisions about corporate strategy and the future business model are being developed, asset portfolio managers should be identifying the strategic decisions relevant to their asset portfolio and begin creating and evaluating alternatives for those decisions.

■ *How can you use divestiture as a means toward achieving your corporate strategy?* As we will discuss shortly, divestiture is an under-utilized management tool. In the course of strategy development, the subject of mergers and acquisitions arises naturally, but not so with divestitures.

Asset Portfolios Must Be Aligned with Financial Measures and Structure

If an investment productivity curve is used independently for each asset portfolio to establish an optimal asset portfolio budget, it is easy to imagine that the sum of these budgets could give a CFO a premature stroke. Aligning balance sheet and cash flow strength with healthy, well-positioned asset portfolios is no small juggling act. To succeed at it you must align the corporate financial performance measures with the performance measures of the asset portfolio so that both the asset portfolio manager and the corporate executives are pursuing the same goals and objectives.

When changing an asset portfolio you should consider these questions about the corporation's financial measures and structure:

■ *Are the performance measures being used by the asset portfolio consistent? Are they directly linked to the primary financial performance measures of the corporation?* To enable the value- and risk-based trade-offs used to maximize overall, system-wide financial performance, you must link the performance measures used for an asset portfolio to the primary financial performance measures of the corporation. If the corporation uses net present value of discounted cash flows to measure corporate financial performance, then each asset portfolio, to the extent possible, should use NPV of discounted cash flow as well.

■ *Are the investment requirements of the asset portfolio coherent and consistent with respect to the comprehensive investment needs across all asset portfolios in the corporation?* The CFO needs to allocate investment across all of the asset portfolios. That is, the CFO is responsible for the "portfolio of asset portfolios." If a single financial measure or a handful of measures are used across all portfolios, the job of the CFO becomes much more manageable. The CEO and CFO can defend an investment in one asset portfolio over another as the best and most appropriate investment strategy.

■ *Are the investment requirements of the asset portfolios aligned with the timing of the targeted changes in the balance sheet and cash flow?* It is inefficient, to say the least, to lay out an asset portfolio strategy only to have it whacked back due to insufficient cash flow and a weak balance sheet. To get this right, corporate finance must work with the asset portfolio managers to communicate the necessary "give and take." Getting the asset portfolios aligned with the corporation's current and envisioned financial structure is an iterative process, not a contentious single event.

Asset Portfolios Must Be Aligned with Organization and Operations

When developing the strategy and changes for an asset portfolio, you must consider the vision for the future state of the organization and operations. The vision obviously impacts equipment and facility assets; more importantly, it also impacts the portfolios of people and competencies.

When changing an asset portfolio, you should consider these questions regarding the organization and operations:

■ *Are the changes in the asset portfolio consistent with the vision of the future organization and operations? If not, how should the asset portfolio changes be adjusted to align with the vision of the future organization and operations?* For example, the future organization and operations may require decision empowerment to be moved down in the organization. Therefore, development and training investments should include training and development in decision quality and efficient decision processes.

■ *Are the long-term investments in the asset portfolio aligned with the vision of the future organization and operations?* One of the authors was once sitting in an office in a building that was to be demolished within the year. He was dumbfounded when he was temporarily moved from his office because it was to be painted. And it didn't even need new paint! Something was dreadfully wrong. Obviously, the facility asset portfolio manager was not working in alignment with the future vision of the organization and operation.

Using Targeted Divestitures as a Management Tool

Most major corporations have a formal function for mergers and acquisitions (M&A) or at least have an M&A team that comes together whenever a merger or acquisition is afoot. Interestingly, corporations do not seem to organize and mobilize the same way when it comes to divestitures, yet divestitures can be just as powerful and value-creating as M&A. Divestitures play an important role in the managing of asset portfolios and, ultimately, the managing of a corporation. Divestitures should be viewed as a management tool, not the unfortunate consequence of a poorly managed asset that must be sold off and booked as a troubling loss.

Successive waves of divestitures have washed over corporations for various reasons. In the 1970s, divestitures increased due to changes in tax laws, recession, and the beginning of the end of conglomerates. In the 1980s and early 1990s, divestitures were driven by the focus on downsizing and rightsizing to align with changing strategies. The current wave of divestitures is being driven by two factors: GAAP changes that eliminate the amortization of goodwill in purchase accounting, and corporations divesting their failed diversification acquisitions made during the 1990s.

Thirty-three percent of acquisitions are ultimately divested, and divested acquisitions are held, on average, seven years. Diversification acquisitions are four times more likely to be divested than nondiversification acquisitions. Over 50 percent of diversification acquisitions are divested. Examples of companies that diversified and subsequently sold many of the acquisitions include ITT, AT&T, Gulf & Western, Tenneco, Westinghouse, Wickes, Teledyne, Litton, Rockwell, and Textron.

The equity market clearly believes that the voluntary selling of a division is a positive development, because it usually rewards the seller with an increase in share price. What results in these situations is reverse synergy, the case where 4 minus 1 equals 5.

Recall the case of Alpha Forest Products discussed earlier. AFP made over 30 acquisitions over a two-year period but never divested a significant asset. After several unsuccessful attempts to resolve performance problems in a recently acquired business unit, worth only about $40 million to $50 million in net present value, the company finally settled on a targeted divestiture of the troublesome unit, and got well over ten times its potential operational value!

Senior executives were recently polled in order to determine their primary motivation for divesting a corporate asset. Some 42 percent of the senior executives claimed that their primary motivation was a "change of focus or corporate strategy." Twenty-eight percent identified their primary motivation as selling in order to "finance acquisition or leveraged restructuring," —the second most common response to the question. And, unfortunately, more than one out of five, or 21 percent, of the executives said that their divestitures were motivated by the unprofitability of the asset or because it was perceived as a mistake. Exhibit 3-12 provides the comprehensive results of the survey.

To turn divestitures into a management tool, you must establish a new perspective on divestitures. Instead of "selling the ashes," you need to know when an asset is worth more to another corporation than to you. A brief case study illustrates this fundamental shift in thinking:

Consider a metal finishing company that has patented a technology and developed an associated system. The metal finishing process that utilizes this technology and system has significantly reduced costs and improved product quality. Moreover, the technology and system replaced a potentially hazardous process with

Exhibit 3-12 – Results of recent survey on motivation for divesting a corporate asset.

a safe, closed system. Originally, the company developed the technology and system in response to a customer. But these innovations aren't considered part of the company's core business nor are they built into the company's strategy for the future. Many defense Original Equipment Manufacturers (OEMs) use similar products that result from this metal finishing process. The metal finishing company has significant debt from a recent management buyout. The company would prefer to sell the technology and system to pay down debt and to use the proceeds to finance an industry consolidation strategy in their core business. They also worry that if they pursue the technology and system on their own, it will distract their management team from their chosen strategy.

When is an asset worth more to a strategic buyer than to the current owner? Strategic buyers include companies that are in competition with the seller, or adjacent to the seller in the same customer value chain (such as a distributor or manufacturer), or in different customer value chains, such as an automotive manufacturer versus a satellite manufacturer.

An asset is worth more to a strategic buyer when the strategic buyer has:

- Immediate access to more markets
- More market applications
- Better strategic fit
- Broader distribution channels
- Better cost structure
- Willingness to commit

In the case of the metal finishing company, a strategic buyer such as a defense OEM could apply the technology worldwide. There are also new market applications, but the metal finishing company lacks the needed capital, management, and facilities. In addition, the system and process could be built into the OEM's plants, which would eliminate shipping and handling charges. Finally, the costs associated with implementing the technology and system are relatively small for an OEM.

Financial buyers/investors constitute a second class of buyers. This includes investment banks, venture capital firms, private equity firms, and business consortia. Although the defense OEMs are interested in one of the system's applications, the OEM lacks the appetite to pursue the many other potential nondefense applications that a financial buyer will pursue. However, financial buyers are typically uninterested in buying or investing in a technology or system alone; they want a management team and an on-going business with revenues.

Whether the buyer is a strategic buyer or a financial buyer, the current owners can get up to ten times the value of the asset in current use. Premiums of this magnitude are achievable when:

- The asset is a scarce resource in a consolidating industry.
- The buyer has the ability to pursue *multiple* new markets.
- The buyer has the ability to pursue *multiple* new market applications.
- The buyer has exclusivity that significantly increases market share and profitability.
- The asset enables the buyer to break through in cost reduction *and* quality.

In the case of the metal finishing company, there exists a strong patent and operational system that could be applied in a severely fragmented industry ripe for consolidation. Market growth is available from North America and worldwide across many defense applications. New market applications exist in other industries, including automotive and consumer goods. Defense OEMs could achieve competitive advantage in cost savings, quality, safety, and environmental compliance. The metal finishing technology and system has all the attributes required to fetch a premium in the marketplace, well above the value to the current owner, the metal finishing company.

Results from our research indicate that, surprisingly, 14 percent of the executives questioned would sell 50 percent or more of the corporation's assets. Exhibit 3-13 presents the results of the complete range of the executives' responses.

Five Key Actions for Getting Big Returns in Asset Divestitures

To get the most from your corporate asset divestitures, there are five key actions your organization should take.

1. *Identify the best divestiture opportunities.* First, consider all of the asset portfolios in the organization including:

- Organizational assets such as business units, divisions, departments, functions, business processes, and sites
- Physical assets such as real estate, plants, large systems, and distribution channels
- Products and services such as intellectual property, concepts, patents, technology, systems, applications, processes, R&D pipeline, and inventory
- People, their skills, knowledge, and competencies

Don't frame this as "Where are the underperforming assets?" but rather as "What assets could be utilized better and contribute more?" Focus on reverse synergy opportunities where 4 minus 1 equals 5. Selling your most valuable asset can be bad or good, as the following two examples from professional baseball show. Ever since the Boston Red Sox traded Babe Ruth in 1919, they have not won a World Series, a result that has become known as the "Curse of the Bambino." On the other hand, the Seattle Mariners traded baseball superstar Alex Rodriguez to the Texas Rangers at the end of the 2000 season. The following season, without

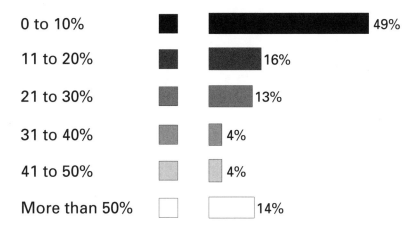

0 to 10%	▮	██████████████ 49%
11 to 20%	▮	████ 16%
21 to 30%	▮	███ 13%
31 to 40%	▮	█ 4%
41 to 50%	▮	█ 4%
More than 50%	▯	▯ 14%

Exhibit 3-13 – Results of recent survey on percentage of corporate assets executives would sell because assets are worth more to another corporation.

Rodriguez, Seattle achieved the best winning percentage in major league baseball with 116 wins and only 46 losses.

The decisions on what to keep, what to sell, what to lease, and what to outsource must always be coordinated and aligned with the corporate strategy, the corporate financial structure, and the organization and operations.

2. *Determine the optimal future use of the asset.* As hockey great Wayne Gretzky advised, "skate to where the puck will be." By pinpointing and measuring the value and risk of future use, you can explicitly understand where the "puck" will be. Exhibit 3-14 illustrates the level of detail required to understand, from the buyer's perspective, the future sources of value for the acquisition of a business unit after it is merged with the buyer's corporation. Exhibit 3-15 illustrates the level of detail required to understand the future sources of risk, also from the buyer's perspective. Understanding, from the buyer's perspective, the sources and magnitudes of value and risk is required to determine the optimal future use of an asset. Basically, you must build the asset into a buyer's strategy or potential strategy and evaluate that strategy.

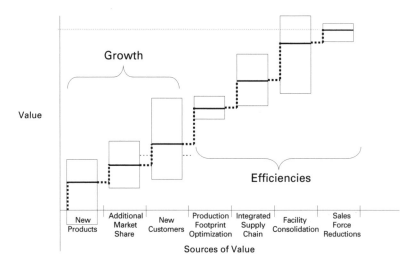

Exhibit 3-14 – Sources and magnitudes of value for the buyer of a business unit.

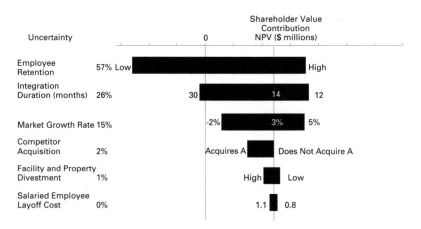

Exhibit 3-15 – Sources and magnitudes of risk for the buyer of a business unit.

Market-pricing approaches often undervalue assets. Standard valuation methods, primarily based on past performance, ignore the future prospect of the asset for a "best buyer." In other words, those methods don't consider completely different uses of the asset. To understand "where the puck will be," you must consider the value of ownership for each specific class of buyer.

3. *Target buyers in the "optimal use" location in the value chain or those getting into that space.* Don't just apply the usual "spray and pray" approach of offering to sell to the usual suspects—namely your current competitors and the companies adjacent to you in the value chain. Consider different classes of strategic buyers, such as companies in entirely different businesses that could significantly benefit from a new marketing and sales channel, a new distribution channel, a new and immediate market presence, improved processes and cost reductions, or a re-branding. Or consider companies with established corporate venturing organizations. At last count, some 38 percent of Fortune 100 companies had corporate venturing, and the number is growing. Over 14 percent of Fortune 500 companies have a corporate venturing organization. And, finally, don't forget the other usual suspects—the financial buyers/investors, such as investment banks, venture capitalists, and business consortia.

4. *Sell from a buyer's point of view.* Make the value proposition crystal clear for the buyer, because they won't do it for themselves. This is not a pro forma of the business under its current ownership. Pinpointing and measuring value and risk is critical when there is no comparable market, as is the case for technology, patents, trade secrets, some physical assets, systems, processes, and machines. Exhibit 3-16 offers the value proposition for a defense OEM for the purchase of the metal finishing technology and system.

5. *Be flexible in the mix of liquidity.* In most cases, the seller wants cash and the buyer wants to minimize the cash component of the deal. Many divestitures involve a combination of compen-

Exhibit 3-16 – Value proposition for a Defense OEM for the purchase of a metal finishing technology and system.

sation forms, including cash, some form of debt instrument, and equity swap. The key here is for the seller to be flexible. Flexibility will lead to maximum divestiture value.

You can significantly influence the value of a divestiture by taking those five actions. The right divestitures multiply your shareholder value returns. Divestiture is a management tool that should be used in a number of different situations to free capital and strengthen your business. Assets that should be divested can be corporate gems or white elephants. The size of the divestiture prize can differ by up to an order of magnitude. But you can make the difference.

CASE STUDY

Alpha Forest Products Gets on the Efficient Frontier

Having uncovered a market- and customer-focused strategy and understood the interdependence of all of the components of value, the AFP team turned its attention to its portfolio of assets. Like most companies, and especially forest products companies, AFP's asset portfolio stood nowhere near the efficient frontier. As we have seen, the efficient frontier is a measure of the relationship between short-term earnings and long-term value creation—in other words, a measure of the optimization of value and risk. But AFP's existing strategy failed to take into account most of the major aspects of value and risk, foreclosing any chance of getting the asset portfolio on the efficient frontier.

In order to move AFP's assets onto the efficient frontier, it was essential to create a matrix of AFP's manufacturing assets versus the products they were capable of making (see Exhibit 3-17). The team analyzed the matrix in three ways:

- What products are the manufacturing organizations producing now?

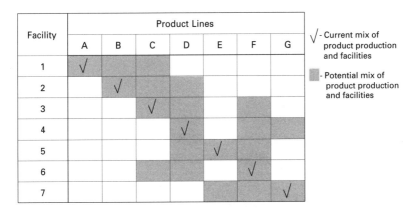

Exhibit 3-17 – AFP's current manufacturing site product production and potential product production allocation.

- What is the entire set of items that each of the manufacturing organizations is capable of producing given their operational equipment and expertise?
- What portfolio of products at this time would produce the greatest value and margins in the marketplace?

As Exhibit 3-18 shows, the results were startling. The analysis demonstrated that:

- Some current products could be made in greater supply by more manufacturing sites.
- Some current products should be abandoned, at least at this particular time.
- Some manufacturing sites should make a completely different mix of products.
- Some manufacturing sites were incapable of manufacturing a winning set of products expected to be in demand in the next three years.

Facility	Product Lines							
	A	B	C	D	E	F	G
1	X						
2		√	X	X			
3			X	X			
4				X			X
5				X	√		
6			X			√	
7							√

√ - Current mix of product production and facilities

- Potential mix of product production and facilities

X - EVA maximizing mix of product production and facilities

Exhibit 3-18 – AFP's EVA, maximizing allocation of products across manufacturing sites.

One of the most valuable insights would have escaped senior management entirely if they had not been looking at their assets from the perspective of the efficient frontier: Some assets were capable of making value-added, high-margin products in spot micro-markets at certain times. But those assets produced product lines sufficiently different so as to lose any advantage in contributing to the ability to create additional product in high-demand times. In other words, some production facilities were really in a different business than the core business.

A strategy that pinpointed new sources of value, the team's changed perceptions of the market, and a desire to move assets accordingly onto the efficient frontier had produced a startling realization: Not all of the production facilities belonged in the mix. The implications were profound. A company that had spent a hundred years acquiring assets did the unthinkable. It began to divest assets. But this was no fire sale. For each asset to be divested, AFP sought a "best buyer," where the asset could move immediately onto that buyer's efficient frontier. The result: The money from the high selling prices of the divested assets was put to work building and buying additional capacity in the core business.

To make all of the trade-offs in products and manufacturing facilities, AFP needed a primary value measure to compare and contrast opportunities. Moreover, AFP needed to ensure that the financial structure of the corporation could support all of the required changes to capture the newly identified sources of value. In the next chapter, we will discuss how AFP addressed the use of financial measures and their financial structure.

Notes

1. Michael S. Allen, *Business Portfolio Management: Valuation, Risk Assessment, and EVA Strategies* (New York: John Wiley & Sons, 2000), p. 2.
2. Harry Markowitz introduced the notion of constructing a portfolio of investments based on expected return and risk as measured by the standard deviation of return. See Harry M. Markowitz, "Portfolio Selection," *Journal of Finance*, March 1952, pp. 77–91.
3. Allen, *Business Portfolio Management.*
4. Jim Matheson and David Matheson, *The Smart Organization* (Boston: Harvard Business School Press, 1998), pp. 202–210.
5. According to legend, the king of Siam gave white elephants to onerous underlords. White elephants were considered sacred; thus they could not be used for labor but required meticulous care and significant upkeep. The burden on the underlords both in time and cost kept them from creating havoc in the kingdom.
6. Paul Sharpe and Tom Keelin, "How SmithKline Beecham Makes Better Resource-Allocation Decisions," *Harvard Business Review*, March–April 1998.
7. Gary Hamel and C. K. Prahalad, *Competing for the Future* (Boston: Harvard Business School Press, 1995).
8. Those interested in this topic should see Mark Ubelhart, "Measuring the Immeasurable," *Shareholder Value*, May–June, 2001, for a value-based methodology for measuring the contribution of human capital.

Financial Measures
and Structure

CHAPTER FOUR

"Measure what is measurable and make measurable what is not so."

—GALILEO GALILEI, ASTRONOMER

As of the fall of 2002, Bill Gates and Microsoft are hoarding cash to the tune of some $40 billion. No other nonfinancial firm has such liquidity at its disposal, and only a few banks do. To put that in perspective, $40 billion could buy the entire airline industry—twice. This huge sum of cash provides a megalithic financial fortress and incredible flexibility in strategy, use, and ownership of assets, and agility in operations. In the past, the accumulation of cash was an indication to investors that the company had stalled in terms of growth opportunities and that dividends should be provided shareholders. Although Microsoft will likely see a sharp decline in sales growth from about 30 percent per year in the 1990s to the mid-teens in the future, there is no plan to turn any part of this cash into dividends. With all the uncertainty in the world and domestic economies, and in this post-

Enron era, not many are complaining and most consider it prudent risk management.

According to John Connors, Microsoft's CFO, the cash will enable significant investment in R&D and allow for long-term equity positions in ventures whenever the opportunity arises— fast and efficiently. Microsoft has taken a position for long-term growth and is successfully positioning itself through the strategic management of its balance sheet and focusing on financial measures for long-term growth and prosperity. So what does this mean for the rest of us who don't have a cash-generating monster like software for personal computers?

Using the right financial measures and right-positioning the financial structure of the corporation is a must for successfully executing strategy, building the right asset portfolios, and creating an agile and responsive organization. Microsoft is an extreme example of leveraging the balance sheet to balance short-term earnings with long-term value creation.

CASE STUDY

Alpha Forest Products Revisits Its Financial Measures and Structure

The senior executives of AFP realized that they needed an organization-wide set of measures that would integrate process productivity, operational effectiveness, and financial outcomes while simultaneously providing insight into specific risks. Moreover, they realized that they needed a single, primary value metric to enable the right discussion on how to trade-off the many alternative product portfolios with manufacturing facility capabilities and organizational capabilities. And to enable the implementation of the changes that would result from this new strategy, the AFP executives realized that they must begin the process of strategically repositioning the financial structure to efficiently capture the strategy's potential value.

The concepts and approaches used for achieving these goals are the topic of this chapter.

The Case for Shareholder Value and Economic Profit Measures

Robert Kaplan and David Norton[1] said it best, "What you measure is what you get." And if you are a for-profit organization, then what you want is growth in shareholder value. So whatever measurement system you use in your organization, you should make sure it is transparently tied to shareholder value. That goes for corporate performance, business unit performance, project performance, capital performance, R&D performance, process performance, and even people performance. Conceptually, it is really that simple. As obvious as this may seem, the trend toward using shareholder value measures and economic profit measures in organizations is a relatively recent one, not entirely embraced, and with a less than stellar track record. Our position is that implementing a shareholder value-based value measure is *necessary* for the alignment of business strategy, asset portfolios, financial measures and structure, and organization and operations; but it is not *sufficient*, as evidenced by corporations that have implemented shareholder value measures but not reaped their benefits.

AT&T began using economic profit measures in 1992 under the guise of a value-based management (VBM) program established to improve their financial performance in a highly competitive and capital-intensive marketplace. By 2000, with no measurable impact on shareholder value, the program was abandoned. According to Haspeslagh, Noda, and Boulos,[2] in contrast to AT&T, the British bank Lloyds TSB, Cadbury Schweppes, Dow Chemical, and Siemens have all claimed significant financial performance improvement through the use of economic profit measures and VBM programs. The chairman of Lloyds TSB, Brian Pitman, was clear on the source of Lloyd's performance improvement: "Doubling the share price every three years can't be accomplished by incremental change; it requires major change and scrapping the old ways of doing things . . . Managing for shareholder value was the driving force behind our success." *Managing* for shareholder value requires *measuring* shareholder value and understanding the impact actions and decisions have on shareholder value.

In simple terms, shareholder value (SHV) of a business equals its present value of future cash flows discounted by its weighted average cost of capital (WACC) less the value of debt. Key to this definition is the notion that a company only creates shareholder value when equity returns exceed equity cost. Most financial experts would agree that *free cash flow* is the cash flow that ultimately matters, because it represents the cash from operations that is readily available to lenders and shareholders. In short, free cash flow represents earnings before interest, tax, depreciation, and amortization (EBITDA) adjusted for changes in working and fixed capital and taxes. The appropriate discount rate to use in calculating the present value of a free cash flow is the weighted average cost of capital (WACC) that accounts for both cost of equity and debt. The tax shield associated with debt is accounted for in the WACC calculation. Detailed definitions and examples of these measures are widely available.[3, 4]

Less obvious is how shareholder value accrues to investors over time in the form of share price. How will the net present value (NPV) of future cash flows manifest itself in this year's stock price, next year's, and so on. Economic profit (EP) was introduced to address this issue. Joel Stern and G. Bennett Stewart introduced "economic value added" (EVA)[5] to do just this. In simple terms, EVA measures the spread between corporate earnings and the cost of capital resources used for a given period, such as a year.

$$EVA = E - WACC \times CE$$

where E is adjusted earnings, WACC is the weighted average cost of capital, and CE is the capital employed for that period.

You must understand the annual impact of decisions and actions on shareholder value for two reasons: communications and performance management. Measuring the EVA of a long-term strategy or change program enables executives to communicate to investors and employees the annual contribution of those initiatives to shareholder value. Because the discounted sum of EVA equals the NPV of the corporation, connections between actions and value can be made crystal clear. And clear, well-timed communications about value enhances the likelihood of an appropriate market response and gives employees a clear sense of their personal contributions to the growing value of the business. By determining quantifiable links between actions and shareholder value, performance measurement and management systems can be designed to ensure that compensation systems incentivize the right behavior for shareholder value growth.

Because the NPV of free cash flow provides a good surrogate measure of shareholder value, it is tempting to look at annual cash flow for annual contributions to shareholder value. Such analysis can provide a reasonable approximation, but it is flawed because generally accepted accounting principles (GAAP) obscure the measurement of annual earnings. Consider the construction of a manufacturing facility. The capital required to construct the facility is depreciated over the productive life of the plant. The reduction in earnings resulting from the investment in the facility is spread over many years.

Contrast this with an R&D investment. According to GAAP, R&D investments are expensed, that is, charged against the earnings of the year in which the expense occurs. Consequently, R&D investments take a much greater toll on current year earnings, which makes them less attractive even though their contribution to shareholder value over time could be much greater. EVA treats all capital expenditures as equal, which eliminates the accounting distortions from GAAP.

The net present value of free cash flows and EVA do have competitors. For over thirty years, executives and financial analysts have scrutinized the relationships among market value, cost of capital, and return on capital investment. A number of measures have been developed for measuring return on capital and are in various degrees of use, including return on equity (ROE), return on investment (ROI), and return on net assets (RONA). Unfortunately, each of these measures completely ignores the size and growth of the corporation, which is essential for the absolute measure of value contribution.

Other competitors include the cash flow return on investment (CFROI) and cash value added (CVA).[6] Our intent is not to state categorically that one SHV measure is superior to all others; however, the NPV of free cash flow and EVA do represent value measurement approaches that enable alignment and ultimately optimization of the decisions and actions across the four components of the value system: business strategy, asset portfolios, financial measures and structure, and organization and operations.

Value measures that enable alignment across the four components of the value system must satisfy the following five principles:

1. *Value measures must ensure logically correct accounting for specific risk*. In a corporate setting, value and risk are inseparable. Consider the sources of uncertainty and risk associated with a new product launch: technical success, patent protection, time to market, staffing requirements, suppliers, competitor actions, changes in consumer preferences, regulations, and economic conditions. Each of these profoundly affects costs, or revenues, and often both. Organizations often go to great lengths in analyzing a new product launch, producing highly detailed forecasts of the new product's performance. But the only thing that is certain about the projected new product financial performance is that it is wrong. With so many uncertain parameters that affect its financial performance, how could it be accurate? Time is spent meticulously estimating each parameter in the forecast of financial performance. The notion of risk is relegated to a qualitative discussion of potential problems, with brief discussions of strategies for mitigating those risks, usually with little or no quantitative supporting evidence. To compensate for the lack of accounting for risk in the financial analysis, the discount rate is often adjusted upward to reflect the "riskiness" of the investment. Does this sound familiar?

There are two fundamental problems with that approach for analyzing the new product launch. First, it focuses on getting the numbers "right" as opposed to understanding which numbers are hard, which are soft, why they are soft, how soft they are, and what could be done to firm them up. Using ranges, instead of point estimates on the parameters impacting the performance of the investment, enables a "learning frame" for discussing and assessing specific risks. Second, adjusting the discount rate upward to reflect the riskiness of the specific investment confuses two separate issues: cost of capital and the specific risk in the investment. In the case of a new product launch, being first to market may be a key element of the product's value potential. Given success in being first to market, the residual risk beyond this event may be relatively low. In that case, it would be inappropriate to continue using the inflated discount rate for the downstream cash flows.

Logically correct accounting of specific risk means that identified risks are quantified with respect to their contribution to uncertainty in cash flow so that the net present value of the cash flow has a probability distribution as opposed to a single point estimate. Only then can we truly understand the impact and value in mitigating the risk in the cash flow.

2. *Use a single value measure, or as few as possible, for the primary value metric.* It is of course easier to align and optimize decisions and actions when there is only one value measure. Once two or more value measures are used then you must understand the preferences in trade-offs among the value measures. How much NPV of cash flow are you willing to give up for near-term market share? How much NPV of cash flow are you willing to give up for safety concerns? How much should you invest in environmental programs? There are no quick and easy rules of thumb here; however, you do need to keep your eye on the ball—shareholder value growth. Always know what you are trading off in terms of your primary metric. Often, issues of safety, hazard, and labor can be treated as constraints rather than as value measures, so the decisions you are left with include whether you want to be "low-side" compliant or "high-side" compliant with respect to the constraints.

3. *Ensure that the primary value metric is directly tied to shareholder value.* Creating and capturing shareholder value is the goal. Make sure that your scorecard has a shareholder value metric as its primary metric. Remember: "What you measure is what you get."

4. *The value measure should enable traceability to decisions and actions.* Every strategic decision and significant action in the organization should be traceable to the value measure. This isn't always easy and certainly isn't required for every decision and action. However, being able to trace decisions and actions to a primary value metric is a key enabler for corporate-wide quality decision-making and performance measurement and management.

5. *The value measure should account for multiyear considerations.* Strategic decisions and actions play out over time periods that typically span several years and, in cases such as oil land leases, over decades. To account for the entire impact of these decisions and actions in terms of shareholder value, you must measure beyond a single period or year.

The Risk-Taking Disconnect

A great disconnect exists between the risk taking of individuals in organizations and risk taking from a shareholder perspective. Consider a business unit leader weighing two strategies for his business unit. As measured in NPV of cash flow, Strategy A has a 40 percent chance of $100 million and a 60 percent chance of negative $20 million. A second strategy, Strategy B, has a 70 percent chance of $5 million and a 30 percent chance of $2 million. Exhibit 4-1 depicts the business unit leader's alternatives.

The expected value of Strategy A is $28 million [(0.40 ×

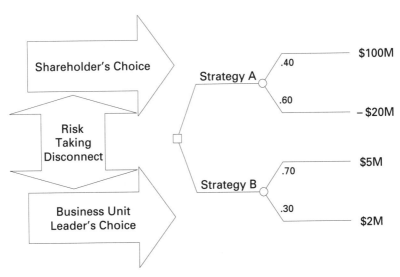

Exhibit 4-1 – A business unit leader's strategic alternatives.

100) + (0.60 × (−20))] and the expected value of Strategy B is $4.1 million [(0.70 × 5) + (0.30 × 2)]. If the business unit leader wanted to delight the shareholders, that leader should line up as many Strategy A-like opportunities as possible. In reality, most organizations are not considering strategies that are as appealing as Strategy A. On the other hand, our experience suggests that most business unit leaders would choose Strategy B over Strategy A. In fact, most business unit leaders would not even introduce Strategy A to the CEO, senior executive committee, or board of directors. Why?

At the heart of the matter is the business unit leader's tolerance for risk. For the corporation at large, succeeding or failing with Strategy A constitutes one bet of many. Playing the odds on Strategy A makes sense because of its overwhelming positive NPV. The shareholders are looking at the expected value as long as the potential loss isn't of the magnitude that it will break the financial back of the corporation. But for the poor business leader, this one strategic decision could make or break a career. The business unit leader fears that racking up a $20 million loss could lead to a one-way ticket down the corporate ladder or out the corporate door. With that much at stake, Strategy A will most likely never be introduced as an alternative. Instead, Strategy B, with its incremental positive return, offers a safe bet with no possibility of loss. As long as Strategy B shows improvement over last year, it looks like a safe, winning choice for the business unit leader.

Getting a Better Handle on Future Cash Flows

The preceding scenario represents a significant problem for corporations. And the bigger the corporation, the more prevalent the problem. Breaking out of this mindset requires executives and managers to have a better handle on value and risk in their decision making. It also requires a cultural transformation with respect to measurement and risk, which we will take up in Chapter 6.

For many businesses, projecting future cash flows is fraught with uncertainty. Consider the cash flow of a single pharmaceutical R&D project, as depicted in Exhibit 4-2. Several uncertainties drive the cash flow of the investment: R&D cost, technical success, whether the drug has blockbuster sales or "me too" sales, competitor actions and products, the duration of sales and peak sales, and many other sources of uncertainty. Ignoring the uncertainty in cash flows or simply applying an increased discount rate as a "fudge factor" simply obscures the underlying cash flow dynamics resulting from the numerous uncertainties.

Cash flows should be managed. Managing requires measuring. By quantifying future cash flow uncertainty and comparing it against financial requirements, financial planning becomes highly proactive. Exhibit 4-3 contrasts uses of cash with uncertainty in cash flow and with financial performance requirements. The question raised in Exhibit 4-3 is, how much cash flow uncer-

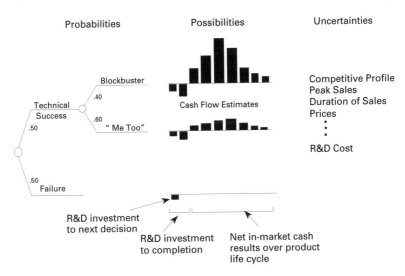

Exhibit 4-2 – Possible cash flow scenarios for a single R&D investment.

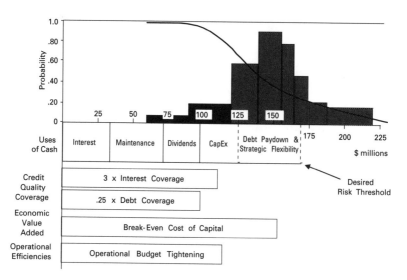

Exhibit 4-3 – Risk profile of cash flow from operations.

tainty can an organization and its shareholders tolerate? By explicitly making decisions on the degree of risk an executive wants to build into plans, planning becomes much more proactive with respect to managing the overall performance of the organization and the risk of achieving the performance targets.

Three perspectives that must be taken into account when you are valuing uncertain or risky cash flows are timing, uncertainty, and degree of aversion to risk. An important and often overlooked distinction is needed here. "Risk" includes uncertainty with respect to information; risk aversion is a preference. Exhibit 4-4 summarizes the relationships of these three perspectives.

Distortions arise when organizations bump up their discount rates to comprehensively account for timing, uncertainty, and risk aversion. The net result is that longer-term value is overpenalized, which makes alternatives that show good short-term value more attractive. As important, the confounding of time and risk preference obscures any insights about specific risks, thus reducing the chances for effective risk management. Exhibit 4-4 sug-

Valuation Dimension	Evaluation Technique	Comment
Timing	Discount cash flow at risk-free rate	Reflects timing preferences only
Uncertainty	Multiply cash flows by probabilities	Reflects state of information, not preferences
Risk Aversion —Capital Markets	Discount cash flow at market cost of capital	Cost of capital combines market preferences on timing and risk
—Corporate	Utility and risk tolerance analysis	Reflects additional corporate concerns about risk, e.g., financial distress

Exhibit 4-4 – The three perspectives that must be taken into account when valuing uncertain or risky cash flows.

gests using utility theory and risk tolerance analysis to account for corporate risk tolerance (preference).[7]

So for strategic decisions that have significant uncertainty, we recommend the following approach:

1. Use an incremental weighted average cost of capital to discount cash flows for time and for capital market risk aversion.

2. Use probabilities to explicitly quantify the major business uncertainties and resulting cash flow scenarios.

3. Use utility theory/corporate risk tolerance in the evaluation when the stakes are large enough to have a major impact on corporate performance.

This approach coherently incorporates both the "systematic" risk concerns of diversified institutional investors (CAPM/cost of capital) and the enterprise risk concerns of running the business (financial distress/corporate risk tolerance). The great advantage of this approach is that it:

- Distinguishes timing, uncertainty, and risk aversion in the cash flow evaluation
- Explicitly captures uncertainty using probabilities
- Quantifies the overall risk profile of cash flow
- Employs utility theory to better capture enterprise risk preference
- Avoids short-term bias and lack of insight from combining timing, uncertainty, and risk aversion into an inflated discount rate

Establishing the Appropriate Risk-Adjusted Cost of Capital

Several key determinants establish a corporation's discount rate or weighted average cost of capital (WACC):

Leverage: The tax advantage of debt encourages companies to use debt financing, but this must be traded off against a higher risk of bankruptcy and the loss of financial flexibility.

Size/Liquidity: The cost of debt and equity is higher for small firms. Over the period from 1926 to 1996, the return on small stocks has averaged about 2 percent higher than for large stocks. Investors in illiquid partnerships, such as venture capital, require still higher returns.

"Beta": The cost of equity is higher for companies whose risk is more strongly correlated with the economy as a whole. Investors cannot diversify this risk by holding a wider range of stocks.

Interest Rates: Higher interest rates raise the nominal cost of capital.

Risk Aversion: If investors are generally feeling more or less risk averse, perhaps due to a general decline or increase in their wealth, then the cost of capital is affected.

Exhibit 4-5 illustrates the blending of cost of equity and cost of debt required to get an appropriate WACC.

Consider an average S&P 500 company. The capital structure of such an organization averages about 75 percent equity and 25 percent debt. The average debt yield is about 5.5 percent and the average effective tax rate is about 38 percent. Let's assume a five-year, risk-free interest rate (such as the return for U.S. Treasuries) that is 5.0 percent. And let's assume the equity risk premium over the five-year risk-free interest rate is 7.3 percent (this is the average difference between stock and Treasury returns over 1926 to 1996). Under these assumptions we have:

$$\text{Cost of equity} = 1.0 \times 7.3\% + 5.0\% = 12.3\%$$
$$\text{Cost of debt} = 5.5\% \times (1 - 0.38) = 3.4\%$$

Consequently, the weighted average cost of capital (WACC) is calculated as:

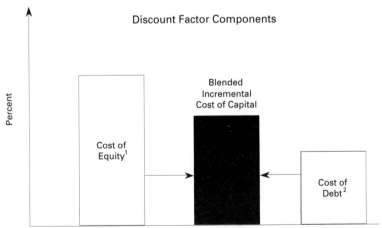

[1] Cost of Equity = Beta x (Expected Equity Premium) + Expected Risk-Free Return
[2] Cost of Debt = Expected Debt Yield x (1–Effective Tax Rate)

Exhibit 4-5 – Establishing a weighted average cost of capital.

$$10.1\% = (0.75 \times 12.3\%) + (0.25 \times 3.4\%)$$

By establishing an appropriate WACC and following the steps discussed in the previous section, you will be well positioned for evaluating cash flows for the purposes of decision making and cash flow management.

Capital Budgeting and Allocation Revisited

Capital budgeting and allocation in most companies is both a bottom-up and top-down process. Exhibit 4-6 illustrates a typical capital budgeting process. There are four classes of capital projects:

1. Projects required by law or corporate policy
2. Maintenance and cost reduction projects
3. Expansion of business projects
4. New products or ventures

From the business units come project proposals for annual capital budgets at the business unit level. At the business unit

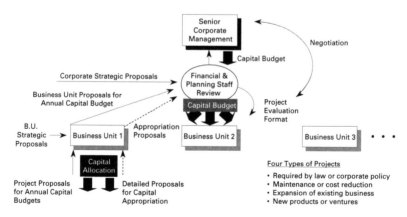

Exhibit 4-6 – Typical capital budgeting and capital allocation process.

level, these capital projects are rationalized and made into a portfolio of projects and submitted to a corporate level function for evaluation and review. These business unit capital project portfolios compete for capital with other business unit project portfolios and the portfolio of corporate strategic proposals. At the corporate level, the overall capital budget is determined and allocated across the business unit and corporate portfolios after negotiation with senior corporate management. The annual capital budget process authorizes funding for projects and the appropriation process approves actual funds.

The goal of capital allocation is easy to state: Get capital to the opportunities promising the highest creation of shareholder value. The challenges to establishing capital budgets and capital allocations include:

- Harnessing decentralized knowledge and information
- Pinpointing and measuring the value potential of capital investments
- Calibrating proposals that have various degrees of optimism in cash flows
- Aligning the corporation's risk tolerance with risk tolerance of managers and staff
- Accounting for risk correctly and consistently throughout the process
- Maximizing the value creation of the overall portfolio of capital projects

Charging business units the opportunity-cost of capital and rewarding value creation will help to overcome these hurdles, but more is needed for a comprehensive solution.

As discussed in Chapter 3, capital projects constitute an asset portfolio, which means that ideas of efficient frontiers and investment productivity fully apply here. To master the challenges of capital budgeting and allocation and improve the financial performance of your corporation's capital investments, you should:

1. *Evaluate capital investments with a shareholder value metric as the primary value measure.* Using additional secondary measures such as return on investment (ROI) is fine. But to compare and contrast the productivity of the individual capital investments you need a shareholder value based metric such as the net present value (NPV) of the discounted cash flows of the capital project. For the discount rate, use the weighted average cost of capital (WACC), as described in the previous section. Uncertainty in the cash flows should be accounted for with probabilities, as opposed to adjusting the discount rate, as described earlier in Exhibit 4-4.

2. *Require the application of decision quality throughout the capital budgeting and capital allocation process.* The six elements of decision quality, introduced in Chapter 2, include: appropriate frame; clear value and trade-offs; meaningful, reliable information; creative, doable alternatives; correct reasoning; and commitment to action. They should all be built into the process.

3. *Allocate capital based on investment productivity.* For example, capital investment productivity for an individual capital project can be defined as the ratio of the change in NPV to the change (or incremental addition) in investment capital. This bang-for-the-buck measure resembles the measure presented in the example on New Business Investment (NBI) in Chapter 3. An investment productivity curve can be created, just as we did in the NBI example. Fund projects with the highest positive capital investment productivity until the corporation or organization hits capital or other constraints. The other constraints may be financial in nature, involve other resource limitations, or depend on the overall corporate risk tolerance for the entire portfolio of capital projects.

4. *Create a formal dialogue across the stakeholders to ensure decision quality.* Building decision quality into the capital budgeting and allocation process requires engaging the key stakeholders in a structured dialogue to ensure that the elements of decision quality are efficiently built into the process. Decision quality should be the defined outcome of the process, not inspected into the process at the conclusion of the process. Matheson and Matheson[8] provide an example of how such a formal dialogue could be structured.

Strategic Management of the Balance Sheet

Strategically managing the balance sheet is as important as managing profit and cash flow. Managing the balance sheet to align it with the other three components of the value system—business strategy, asset portfolios, and organization and operations—is a tricky game. But creating a balance sheet that enables change across these three components, as opposed to impeding change, is the reward. Asset turnover and leverage are the two balance sheet metrics that drive the power of the balance sheet and enable change.

The basic techniques for improving asset turnover include:

- Operating with as little cash as possible and returning surplus cash to the owners, by paying dividends or executing stock buybacks
- Reducing days sales outstanding (DSO)
- Reducing inventory days
- Divesting assets that are idle, under-utilized, or that are keeping the asset portfolio off of the efficient frontier
- Ensuring that all retained assets have returns at least as great as the WACC

Corporations increase their leverage by using more borrowed money to run operations. The tax advantage of using borrowed money is weighed against the financial risk of cash flows being insufficient to cover debt payments, as depicted in Exhibit 4-3.

Strategic management of the balance sheet—that is, strategically positioning the balance sheet for future change—is done through a combination of five actions: asset securitization, strategic refinancing, stock buybacks, targeted divestiture, and corporate venturing.

Asset Securitization

Asset securitization is the act of selling an asset to an entity in the form of a trust. The trust pays the company for the asset and the trust receives capital by selling positions in the trust's future cash flow. The company benefits from the securitization when the asset is creating relatively low earnings. The asset securitization takes the asset off of the balance sheet and replaces it with cash that can be strategically reinvested into one or more of the other three value components; or the cash can be given back to the shareholders. Because almost any asset that has regular cash flow can be securitized, you can be creative here. Financial companies securitize loans receivable. Manufacturers, distribution companies, and service companies securitize receivables.

Securing private equity funding through a partnership to launch or grow a spin-off business is gaining popularity. By reorganizing into discrete business units, you can sell equity positions to strategic partners, venture capitalists, or equity partners. Although asset securitization is becoming an ever more popular balance sheet lever, it is only one of five actions that can be taken to strategically manage the balance sheet.

Strategic Refinancing

Strategic refinancing requires that you assess the inherent uncertainty in interest rates. With relation to current rates, you must assess whether interest rates will be going up or down over the next two to four years.

If your assessment indicates that rates will be trending downward during this time, then you should borrow in the short-term with the intent to roll over the debt within the year. Commercial paper, unsecured notes issued by companies and maturing within nine months, typically offers the least expensive form of debt available. As interest rates decline over the year, you will be rolling over the debt to a lower rate at each stage of refinancing. Additionally, you should consider swapping any fixed rate debt over to variable rate debt to enjoy further savings as the rates slide down over the time period.

On the other hand, if the assessment indicates that rates will be trending upward during this period, then two actions become viable and can be done in conjunction: One, borrow long-term on a fixed rate basis, and two, pursue interest rate swaps to swap out any variable debt for fixed rate debt.

Obviously, strategic refinancing carries risk. Incorrectly assessing interest rate trends will cost you.

Stock Buybacks

Stock buybacks regularly make headlines in the business sections of newspapers. Big players like General Motors, IBM, and Microsoft have all recently executed this strategic balance sheet action. For the most part, two methods for implementing stock buybacks have been used: purchasing stock through the open market and Dutch auctions.

A stock buyback impacts the financial framework of the company in several ways:

- Earnings per share increase since less stock is outstanding.
- The weighted average cost of capital (WACC) decreases.
- If the stock is utilized to satisfy employee stock option grants and contracts, then dilution is completely avoided.

Targeted Divestiture

Targeted divestiture should be considered for any asset that is worth more to another entity than it is worth to the current owner, as discussed in detail in Chapter 3.

Corporate Venturing

More and more corporations are establishing venture capital programs and organizations. At last count, thirty-eight corporations in the Fortune 100 had internal venture capital programs and 14 percent of the corporations in the Fortune 500 have such programs and organizations. These corporations are spread across many industries and include AT&T, American Express, Chevron, Dell, Dow Chemical, General Electric, Johnson & Johnson, Motorola, and UPS.

Through corporate venturing, organizations can participate in a broader range of potential future markets, products, and services by partnering in investment, leveraging internal assets (plants, processes, competencies, intellectual property, etc.), and sharing the risk and return of these ventures. Managing the portfolio of corporate venture initiatives is, yet again, managing an *asset portfolio,* requiring application of the techniques detailed in Chapter 3.

By strategically combining the five actions of asset securitization, strategic refinancing, stock buybacks, targeted divestiture, and corporate venturing, the CFO can optimally position the corporation's balance sheet to enable change across the entire value system.

Financial Measures and Structure Must Be Aligned with Organization and Operations

Chapter 2 examined the questions that must be addressed in aligning business strategy with financial measures and structure. Chapter 3 presented the questions that must be addressed in aligning asset portfolios with financial measures and structure. Whenever there are discussions involving making changes in financial measurement, or restructuring the balance sheet, or managing cash flow differently, all of those questions should be revisited. This section takes up the questions that should be addressed in aligning financial measures and structure with organization and operations.

For the most part, the key in aligning finance with operations is getting alignment among measurements, incentives, and the balance sheet. To achieve these alignments you must address these questions:

■ *Do the operational performance measures drive the primary financial value measures?* In an ideal setting, all the operational performance measures used in an organization would have quantifiable relationships (not necessarily cause and effect) with the primary measure of shareholder value. The change in shareholder value for changes in process improvement would then be calculable. Although this degree of clarity about the relationship is achievable, it is not practical. Short of this, it is possible to understand the *directional* relationship between almost any operational measure and NPV of cash flow or EVA. First, you must ensure that none of the measures used in the organization promote actions or decisions that destroy shareholder value. Second, you should complete an analysis that identifies the key drivers of value creation for the organization.

Once these drivers are identified, you can create a linked network of performance measures that are directionally aligned with the primary financial measures. Even better, you can create a linked network of performance measures that have quantifiable relationships with the primary financial performance measures for the value drivers of the business.

■ *Does the compensation and incentive system drive the right behaviors, actions, and decisions in staff to maximize the primary value measures?* If you are being compensated for volume, as opposed to value, there could be a problem. In many industries and organizations, more volume does not necessarily imply more shareholder value. Ideally, you should understand how each role contributes to shareholder value creation. Again, although this is possible, it is not practical to implement. If all of the operational measures are aligned with shareholder value creation, and if incentive systems are based on operational performance measures, then there is no issue. At a minimum, each organization should ensure that there are no incentive and compensation policies that destroy shareholder value creation.

■ *Is the risk tolerance of the corporation reflected in individual investment decisions being made across organizations?* All organizations have the inherent problem of individuals making decisions based on their personal tolerance for risk as opposed to the corporation's tolerance for risk. Building decision quality, as defined in Chapter 2, into the strategic decision processes of an organization helps mitigate the problem by ensuring that significantly different alternatives have been created and evaluated before each key decision is made.

■ *Has the uncertainty in cost of operations been accurately reflected in the cash flow risk assessment?* Exhibit 4-3 depicts the notion that cash flow in a given year is uncertain. By quantifying the uncertainty in each of the components that determine cash flow, such as cost of operations, you can set budgets that determine how likely it is that cash flow will cover the needs of the corporation. In essence, senior executives get to precisely dial-in the degree of risk in having a cash flow shortfall. Do you want to have a 90 percent chance of funding all strategic initiatives or a 50 percent chance (see Exhibit 4-3). If the uncertainty in cash flow is not measured, you are left guessing and get stuck in circular debates about sufficiency in cash flow.

■ *Do the cash flow and balance sheet enable the changes that should be pursued in the organization and operations?*

There is nothing worse for a COO than to have an insightful vision for the organization only to find that the vision cannot be appropriately pursued due to cash flow and balance sheet constraints. Worse yet, pursuing this vision in the face of cash flow and balance sheet constraints only to fail in the implementation lowers employee morale. "Here we go again," they say, "another failed attempt at change." Organizational change must be aligned with the overall financial situation of the organization. Moreover, cash flow and the balance sheet must be at least one step ahead of organizational change, ensuring that financing enables, rather than impedes, change.

■ *Does the capital budgeting and allocation process ensure that the most value adding initiatives are funded?* Capital projects represent an asset portfolio. Consequently, making sure the capital projects constitute an efficient portfolio of projects is a must. The work of creating an efficient portfolio of capital projects will ensure that the most value adding initiatives are funded with appropriate weight given to near-term gains versus long-term value creation.

■ *Should a corporate venture program or organization be established to better leverage assets and create a broader set of opportunities?* It is hard to argue against such an idea. Leveraging your existing assets more effectively, reducing investment exposure, pursuing a broader set of opportunities, sharing the risk and return—there's nothing wrong with that. If you don't have the staff to run such an organization, then you should consider acquiring them.

CASE STUDY

Alpha Forest Products and Financial Measures

The management of Alpha Forest Products had a clear direction: They were going to move from a bottom-rung, poor-performer (as measured in total shareholder return) in a low-margin commodity business with an operations-focused strategy, to a high performing market- and customer-based organization in a high-margin business. And they knew what they had to do: Optimize their portfolio of assets, move it onto an efficient frontier, and keep expanding the frontier.

But how to measure? The AFP management team decided that they needed an organization-wide set of measures that integrated process productivity, operational effectiveness, management accomplishments, and financial outcomes. But most importantly, they believed that they needed a single overriding financial measure for the entire system of value.

AFP chose EVA as their primary and universal financial measure. EVA became ubiquitous in the organization. All employees at all levels in all departments in all product lines used EVA as the major criterion in decision making.

It didn't matter whether a product or service idea percolated up from a first-level supervisor to senior management, or whether, conversely, a directive came down from senior management to middle- and first-level management. In both cases, as in all cases, EVA became the common vocabulary, both conceptually and actually.

This single financial measure, used at all levels, soon became part of the collective consciousness of the organization. It was accepted because it was understandable, it was credible, it spoke to the major problem—the fact that they never made their cost of capital—and it was fair in its company-wide application.

EVA was also considered a good choice because it had a direct and underlying linkage to financial performance and even financial structure. Since the EVA calculation incorporates an understanding of the accounting systems as well as the cost of capital, it is a measure both of financial performance and of financial structure.

AFP was satisfied that EVA aligned with their strategy of pinpointing and measuring sources of value and determining the expected value in the face of risk and uncertainty. It also helped guide their asset portfolio optimization by helping to measure the contribution of assets with respect to the efficient frontier. As mentioned in Chapter 3, a business unit of AFP pursued a targeted divestiture that both repositioned AFP with respect to its efficient frontier, but also strategically repositioned the balance sheet to finance the changes they needed to undertake. And, as we will see in Chapter 5, the use of an EVA performance measurement system forced a forward look into the operational and organizational issues.

Notes

1. R.S. Kaplan and D.P. Norton, "The Balanced Scorecard: Measures That Drive Performance," *Harvard Business Review*, January–February 1992, pp. 71–79.
2. Philippe Haspeslagh, Tomo Noda, and Fares Boulos, "Managing for Value: It's Not Just About the Numbers," *Harvard Business Review*, July–August 2001, pp. 65–73.

3. Richard Brealey, Stewart Myers, *Principles of Corporate Finance* (New York: McGraw-Hill, 1996).

4. Andrew Black, Phillip Wright, and John Davies, *In Search of Shareholder Value: Managing the Drivers of Performance*, 2nd edition (London: *Financial Times* and Prentice Hall, 2001).

5. G. Bennett Stewart, *The Quest for Value* (New York: Harper Business, 1991).

6. For an analysis of these measures see Black, Wright, and Davies, *In Search of Shareholder Value.*

7. For an overview of dealing with corporate risk tolerance and utility, see Robert T. Clement and Terence Reilly, *Making Hard Decisions*, 2nd edition (New York: Duxbury Press, 2001), pp. 527–546.

8. Jim Matheson and David Matheson, *The Smart Organization* (Boston: Harvard Business School Press, 1998), pp. 176–180.

Organization and Operations

CHAPTER FIVE

"The mistakes are all waiting to be made."

—CHESSMASTER SAVIELLY GRIGORIEVITCH TARAKOWER (1887–1956), ON THE
GAME'S OPENING POSITION

When Lou Gerstner became chairman of the board and chief executive officer of IBM in 1993, he made it clear that "Big Blue" didn't need more work and effort in strategy, but that their focus should be on execution. This change in focus coupled with Gerstner's leadership and winning strategy have led IBM to spectacular gains in stock price, including two stock splits in his tenure. In our experience, corporations are not starved for good ideas and opportunities. It is the pursuit of the changes required to capture the value associated with these ideas and opportunities where corporations stumble. Gerstner was acutely aware of this and forced the focus on IBM's organization and operations.

CASE STUDY

Alpha Forest Products Needs an Organizational and Operations Overhaul

The challenge for AFP was moving from low-margin commodities to higher-margin, higher-value products, which required an overhaul of the organization and operations. The overhaul must change AFP from an operational excellence focus to a market- and customer-facing company with focus on product leadership and customer relationships. Radical changes would be required in work processes, reporting relationships, decision empowerment, information systems, roles and responsibilities, and more. The types and degree of change were overwhelming to the executives. They had never implemented anything so radically different in the history of the business. Should they even try?

Well try they did. And the results surprised even the optimists. This chapter presents the approaches used by AFP to make the needed changes to their organization and operations.

The Legacy of Gus and Joe

In the late 1990s, we came upon a large, multibillion dollar, publicly-held manufacturing organization that was having great financial difficulty. A careful study of the company showed an organization totally out of alignment with business strategy, asset portfolios, and financial measures and structure. But more significantly, the organization defied all attempts at rational management explanation.

The organization chart (Exhibit 5-1) looked as if it had been designed to test whether any processes could so be shaped, extended, splintered, and convoluted as to be able to make it through the entire organizational maze. It was particularly fascinating because the company was public. The organization chart, a remnant of the company's early days as a private organization, had remained intact through an IPO many years earlier and had survived to almost the turn of the twenty-first century.

And so it was with great anticipation that we prepared to meet with the chairman and CEO, the son of the man who had founded the organization some forty years earlier. The discussion with the CEO focused almost immediately on the dysfunctional organizational structure. Not only did the organization suboptimize the delivery of revenue and profitability, but also it actually impeded the company's ability to perform. Organizational components that naturally performed and worked best together stood at opposite ends of the company. Reporting relationships defied management logic and theory—it was simply the most ill-designed and suboptimizing organizational design we had ever seen. And so we asked the CEO: "How did you select this organizational design for your company?" Without hesitation the CEO replied, "It was because of Gus and Joe."

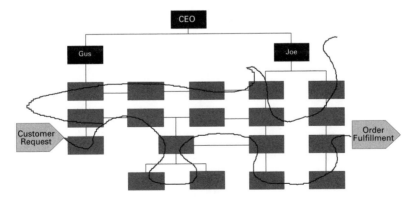

Exhibit 5-1 – The legacy of Gus and Joe.

In the early days of the company—as a private manufacturing firm in the late 1950s—Gus and Joe were two of the key managers in the organization. As the company grew from a start-up, Gus and Joe—who had, at best, only tolerated each other—developed a relationship that bordered on mutual contempt. Eventually, they came to detest each other. Yet the founder had felt that Gus and Joe were each vital to the success of the growing enterprise. So, in 1963, he designed the organization around Gus and Joe, dividing up the organizational units in ways that would create less interaction and conflict between them. For years afterward, the company limped along, growing revenue and profitability only incrementally by working around this artificial organizational design, meanwhile sacrificing billions of dollars of shareholder value.

When we asked the obvious question, "What happened to Gus and Joe?" we were told that "Gus retired in 1969, and Joe died in 1970." And yet for almost three decades since, the organizational design had remained unchanged.

Incredible as it seems, this story is true. And it points to a larger truth: Most organizations are artifacts of a vanished world. They were designed at a different time, for different reasons, around different people, for different markets, and with different ends in mind. And when we dig up their pasts—as we did in this case—we often find something like the story of Gus and Joe. More importantly, we unearth their legacy: the squandering of billions of dollars of shareholder value.

As our research shows, the spirit of Gus and Joe remains alive and well in today's organizations. To reiterate our key findings:

- Sixty-eight percent of senior executives report that their organizational design and structure actually impede their strategy and their ability to deliver value.
- Fifty percent of senior executives report that their organizations are unable to respond to changes in their markets, the supply chain, or their value chain.

■ Twenty-five percent represents the size of the gap between the organizational capability the executives say they require to run their businesses and the organizational capability they actually have.

■ Forty percent equals the amount of strategic value that senior executives report squandered by companies whose organization and operations are misaligned with the other three components of value: business strategy, asset portfolios, and financial measures and structure.

Although the story of Gus and Joe represents perhaps the most extreme case of organizational dysfunction, the figures suggest that something like their story may be more the rule than the exception among organizations today. Quite simply, organizations are letting massive amounts of value leak away.

Many organizations have merely evolved in much the same way as portrayed in the story of Gus and Joe. And when organizational structures are changed, the opportunity for creating real value gets away: Organizational boxes are shuffled, people are reassigned, victory is proclaimed, centralized organizations are decentralized, and decentralized organizations are recentralized; the event becomes a world-wide corporate communications opportunity, and yet in both the short run and the long run, the center cannot hold. And massive amounts of value continue to leak away.

Something's Happening Here—What It Is Ain't Exactly Clear

No one sets out to fail, and certainly not on such a massive scale. Yet, collectively, in organizations, executives and managers build failure into the system. Worse, even after the inadequacies of the system become painfully apparent, those in charge stubbornly resist doing anything about it. Why?

An in-depth analysis of organizational dysfunction at a major automaker produced some extremely provocative answers. Interestingly, senior executives already knew those answers. Both the analysis and the executives identified the three major causes of organizational misalignment and misdesign at the company:

1. *Cultural Intractability:* The company constantly and universally promoted innovation, except when it touched on organizational design. Innovation died at the front door of organizational structure.

2. *Gaming the System:* Major organizational changes or improvement initiatives were actually manipulated in order to ensure the survival of organizational "sacred cows."

3. *Operational Impotence:* Even when the company intended to foster major organizational rethinking and redesign, the people responsible for implementing the changes lacked the power, authority, and cross-functional span-of-control required to move the organizational design changes from strategic concept to reality.

These three factors—cultural intractability, gaming the system, and operational impotence—often make many organizations into immovable objects. Overcoming them requires an irresistible force in the form of strong-willed leadership focused on optimizing the value delivered by the corporation.

The challenge for the leader is great—taking on something as big, as complex, and as resistant to change as an entire organization. But the opportunity is even greater: aligning the organization with the other interdependent components of the value system in order to maximize the creation of value. After all, it is through the organization—and the operational engine that it both contains and enables—that value is delivered. That is where the other components of the value system find their realization—in organizational performance.

Making It Work

In addition to a strong will, the leader will need to either thoroughly understand what it takes to redesign an organization or seek the assistance of someone who does. Unfortunately, many leaders mistakenly believe that they already understand what it takes. Consider that the majority of American corporations take *one-time* restructuring charges *every year*—clearly a contradiction. Does this continued shuffling and reshuffling of organizational units and boxes result from the companies having acted too quickly? Too slowly? No, it results from approaches to organizational design that are often both simple and simplistic. The corporate leaders underestimate the relative complexity of the undertaking; they ignore the need for quantitative measurement; they lack the skill for large-scale change management. It all appears to be very easy: Do it and get it over with.

But designing or redesigning an organization in order to improve or to optimize operational performance is very much a process rather than an event. And the process must be clear, proven, and actionable if it is to optimize the organizational/operational engine of the corporation and enable it to deliver maximum value. Exhibit 5-2 shows just such a process, involving five critical action steps:

1. Align
2. Define
3. Design
4. Commit
5. Build

Each of the steps has a toolset, an agenda of activities, and clear deliverables. Most importantly, each step is guided by the overriding principle of managing value as a system: Organizational design is treated as an interdependent component of value,

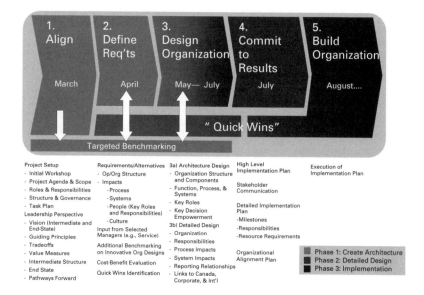

Exhibit 5-2 – The five critical action steps of optimizing operational performance.

whose ultimate value derives from its relationship with business strategy, asset portfolios, and financial measures and structure.

Step One: Align

Alignment focuses on ensuring that senior management shares a clear, consistent, concrete, and creative idea of what they want to achieve and that they individually and mutually remain committed to taking action. Everyone understands the organization that they are trying to build and what they are trying to achieve in building it.

At this stage, leaders must gain a shared perspective about:

■ Vision, mission, and strategy
■ Issues and challenges
■ Primary goals
■ Core values and operating principles

Alignment begins with an explicit discussion of the corporate vision, mission, goals, and values. It moves from a common and shared understanding of these high-level principles to a specific understanding and agreement upon the answer to the central question of strategy: what is the optimal destination for our corporation and what's the best road to get there?

In 80 percent of the cases that we have been actively involved in and have analyzed, each member of a corporation's management team believed that she had a clear and consistent idea of the vision and strategy of the corporation. As it turned out in these cases, however, the executives each had a different and often mutually exclusive idea of the vision and strategy of the firm. Moreover, they did not openly discuss or communicate the differences. These potentially disastrous differences were discovered only through exercises like the following case.

Case Study: Quick Check on Organizational Alignment

The CEO of a major U.S. polymer company and his nine direct reports, in anticipation of a major organizational redesign, were each asked to provide two different scores on two sides of an index card. On side A, with ten as the highest possible score and zero as the lowest, they were asked to record the number that they felt best indicated their understanding of alignment with, and commitment to, the company's overall strategy and direction. On side B, they were asked to record the number that best described their belief that no matter what, the CEO would implement some major new organizational redesign by year's end.

The results were quite remarkable. Side A—how well do you really understand and are committed to the corporate strategy and direction—produced an average score of three out of the possible ten. Only the CEO, as it turned out, had scored it nine. On the B side of the card—how certain are you that the CEO will push through some organizational redesign soon—the average score was nine. Net net: We have no understanding of our direction or the requirements it will place on our organization, but we are certain that we will take significant action now. Motion, not action. Chaos, not alignment. There's something happening here, but what it is ain't exactly clear.

Begin with the End in Mind

Beginning with the end in mind—popularized by Steven Covey's *The Seven Habits of Highly Effective People*—has long been a staple of systems thinking. In the Align step of organizational design, as seen in Exhibit 5-3, there are three essential tasks:

1. Identify a vision of the optimized future state.

2. Agree on the current state from a systems perspective, including the relationships of business strategy, asset portfolios, financial measures and structure, and operations and organization.

3. Identify the business and technical challenges of closing the gap from the current state to the desired optimized future state.

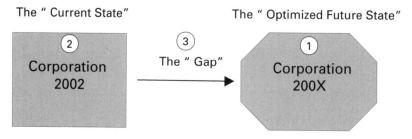

Exhibit 5-3 – The three essential tasks of organizational design.

To best accomplish these three alignment tasks, it is useful to develop a decision hierarchy, as shown in Exhibit 5-4. The decision hierarchy, a tool that helps a group to work optimally in considering critical pathways to the best organizational design, breaks the decisions down as follows:

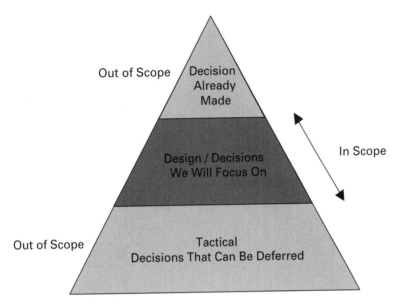

Exhibit 5-4 – Decision hierarchy.

- The givens; decisions that are already made that will not be changed by this project
- Organizational design decisions that will be the focus and subject of this project
- Tactical decisions that can be deferred for later consideration following the outcome of this project

Exhibits 5-5, 5-6, and 5-7 provide an example of a decision hierarchy. It is essential to distinguish precisely what decisions need to be made later in the process in order to deliver a working model of our idealized vision of the end state. In practical terms, using a decision hierarchy keeps us focused. If it is a given that we are going to remain in the manufacturing business, then it wastes valuable time to consider organizational structures that would transform the company into a service business. However, if the manufacturing-to-service transition is an open strategic question, then a good deal of organizational design consideration

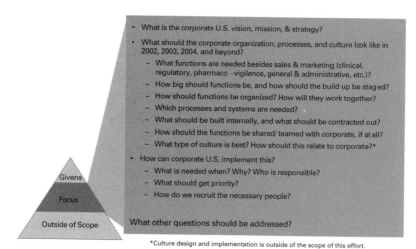

Exhibit 5-5 – Decision hierarchy: Example A.

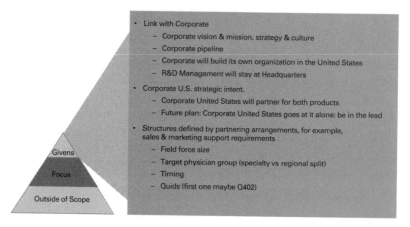

Exhibit 5-6 – Decision hierarchy: Example B.

may go here. Understanding the givens helps harness the attention necessary to get full value from the alignment step of organizational design.

The decision hierarchy also prevents us from getting bogged-down in unnecessary tactical details. In the early stages of organizational design the choice of a particular brand of computer or a

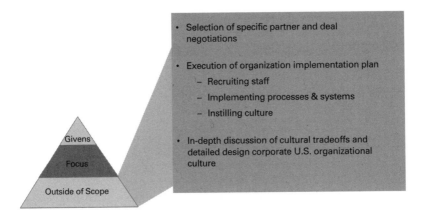

Exhibit 5-7 – Decision hierarchy: Example C.

software solution is not required. However, leaders often feel that unless they can solve everything at once, they can do nothing at all. And so paralysis can ensue when the boundary between strategic elements of organizational design and their tactical expression blurs.

We once had a colleague who, by age 24, had been graduated *summa cum laude,* had been valedictorian and Phi Beta Kappa, had won Woodrow Wilson, Fulbright, and Rockefeller Foundation scholarships, and had completed all but his dissertation for his doctorate at Yale. Twenty years later, with his dissertation still unfinished, he was no longer a prodigy but a poor journeyman instructor at community colleges. Asked why he had never finished his work, he replied: "I had so much to say that I wanted to say everything; I ended up saying nothing."

By sharply focusing our attention and energy in the alignment stage, the decision hierarchy helps us avoid the pitfall of feeling that we have to do everything at the start. In addition to helping us identify the givens that we can't change, it also helps us distinguish the tactics—the elements of in-depth implementation that will follow from our work—that do not need to be determined at the outset. As a result, we can devote full attention to the real organizational design work—what we need to decide now.

Beginning with the end in mind, then, means that we need to develop, during the Align step, a description of our mutual and aligned aspiration for the company at some point in the future. Usually we're looking three to five years into the future, and we're trying to develop a clear, consistent, coherent, and common description of how our organization will look and function at that time.

The deliverable items from the Align step are shown in Exhibit 5-8. In order to successfully develop these deliverable outputs, it is important for the corporate team that is working this problem to develop two key project tools:

- The entire project will be clearly defined in a presentation format that will detail:

    —Project Agenda and Scope: What will be accomplished and what is not part of this project that needs to be accomplished later

    —Roles and Responsibilities: By name and role, what responsibilities each will have in this project

    —Structure and Governance: A detailed description of how executive leadership, the steering committee, and the project team will communicate, identify, and resolve issues; make decisions; and align the broader organization to this U.S. launch

    —Project Plan: A detailed plan in the form of a Gantt chart defining the work activities, responsibilities, timing, and dependence of activities

- A second document in a presentation format will detail:

    —The vision, mission, and primary goals of the project and U.S. launch

    —The issues, challenges, and risks in the launch

    —The strategies for resolving critical issues and risks

    —The core values and operating principles that will guide behaviors and actions on the project and for the resultant U.S. organization

---

Exhibit 5-8 – The deliverable items from the Align step.

■ *A Project Charter:* The operational design team must charter a set of core values (Exhibit 5-9A) and operating principles by which they will conduct the project. This project charter (Exhibit 5-9B) is essential for the full and frank conversations necessary to ensure that the organizational design is undertaken as an interdependent component of a value system that must include business strategy, asset portfolios, and financial measures and structure.

■ *Targeted Benchmarking:* The organizational design team must conduct a "targeted benchmarking" effort that produces a catalog of high-quality organizational design options. Targeted benchmarking differs from conventional benchmarking in one critical respect: Targeted benchmarking establishes a correlation between organizational design and total shareholder value, and seeks an understanding of those organizational elements that can make the difference between average performance and breakthrough performance by a company in a market, in an industry, in a product setting, or any other competitive environment. Targeted benchmarking avoids the "so what?" syndrome that has so often resulted in the pointless accumulation of comparative materials in benchmarking exercises over the past fifteen years.

In the Align step, we only begin targeted benchmarking; it continues throughout most of the four steps of the organizational design project. What is important during the Align step is to make a wise and deliberate selection of a half a dozen to a dozen organizations to study. The selection of these targeted benchmarks derives from work with a decision hierarchy: What precisely are the organizational elements under consideration and what is our vision of an optimized future state three to five years from now? The targeted benchmarking work that begins here in the Align step will be put to good use in the Define and Design steps that follow.

• Participation	• Reliability
• Honesty	• Openness (Open Mind)
• Quality	• Fun
• Respect	• Empathy
• Equality	• Support
• Commitment	• Integrity
• Dedication	• Sincerity
• Timeliness	• Passion
• Diversity	• Humor
• Success	• Trust
• Accountability	

Exhibit 5-9A – Core values.

- Fulfill commitments
- Ask for help if needed
- Respect each individual, especially in disagreement
- Challenge ideas, not individuals (Remember, nothing is personal)
- Support and communicate the work of the team out to the workplace
- No distinction between job titles
- Constructive participation is required
- Be willing to compromise
- Stand united on issues (Support team direction; if not, work to resolve conflict)
- Listen to each other
- Each individual is responsible to keep up and stay informed
- Team must support the development of individuals
- Inform sub-team leader one day in advance if you plan to miss a meeting
- The only stupid question is one without an answer
- Bring in a big picture perspective
- Celebrate success!

Exhibit 5-9B – Operational design team charter.

Step Two: Define

Make everything as simple as possible, but not simpler.

—ALBERT EINSTEIN, AMERICAN PHYSICIST

At the Define step we begin to make critical decisions about the organizational system that we are going to design. Recall that the Align step produced a detailed description of the optimized future state as well as of the gap between that future state and where we are today. The Define step is where "the rubber meets the road."

A simple example from the realm of personal experience helps clarify the distinctions between Align, Define, and Design:

■ *Step 1, Align:* Five years from now, we would like to be in a 5,000 square foot house, on a substantial piece of property near the water with good access to work, educational, and commercial opportunities. We live now in an urban community in a 1,500 square foot co-op and we work in a company that provides us little long-term growth, but in a profession that provides significant mobility.

■ *Step 2, Define:* In this step we make the specific decisions that issue from the definition that came out of our alignment work. These decisions include selecting community, a style of house, a piece of land, etc. But these decisions must be viewed as interdependent components, since the value of this aligned vision comes from the entire experience, not from just the house, or just the land, or just the community, or just the location. This set of decisions must be internally consistent. Similarly, as we have seen earlier, organizational design decisions must be internally consistent with each other and with all other elements of the value system.

■ *Step 3, Design:* In this step, we make a further set of decisions about specific details. Once we have selected the style of house in Define—Victorian, colonial, split-level, raised ranch,

Georgian—we now specify roofing, doors, windows, flow, etc. Those choices can only be made after the style of house has been defined.

Simply put, *Align* is the description of what we want, *Define* is choosing the high-level system we want, and *Design* is specifying the specific components of what we want. Too often, corporations and organizations move directly to selecting an organizational design without considering and understanding the full range of options—and the correlation between those design decisions and the production of shareholder value.

Just as decision hierarchies aid the Align phase, numerous tools exist to help a project team optimize its decisions during the Define step, including:

- The congruence diagram
- Decision tables
- Qualitative and quantitative tools

The Congruence Diagram

The congruence diagram provides a major tool for working toward making the best possible organizational design decisions. Shown in Exhibit 5-10, the congruence diagram is used to detail the decisions in the Define step that issue from the idealized vi-

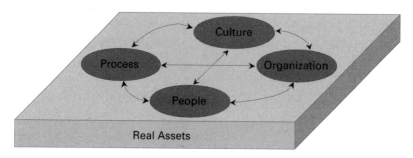

Exhibit 5-10 – The congruence diagram.

sion of the future state and from the decision hierarchy that emerged in the Align step. Recall that in Align, we use the decision hierarchy to separate: (1) decisions that are givens, (2) specific decisions that need to be made in the consideration of this organizational design project, and (3) tactical decisions that will eventually follow from our other decisions. Recall also that we began with the end in mind, and thereby *described* a vision of the organization in the future that would best align with the other components of corporate value. The congruence diagram provides a way of thinking about the specific organizational components that we need to make decisions about in the Define step.

The entire congruence diagram appears when we "double click" on organization and operations as part of our larger value system (as shown in Exhibit 5-11). And we get even further detail when we deconstruct our organization/operations into its component parts (see Exhibit 5-12). Now we can take a deeper look at the congruence diagram and the four major components, each of

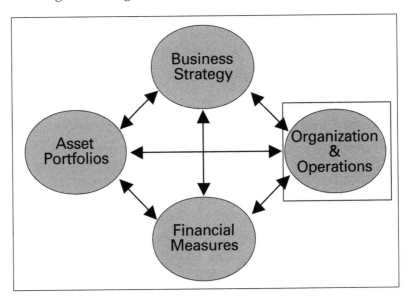

Exhibit 5-11 – Congruence is part of a larger value system.

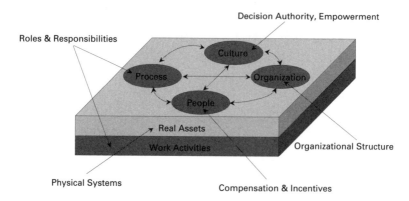

Exhibit 5-12 – Changes to organization/operations requires a broad perspective.

which has relationships to all of the other components ("bubbles") shown in Exhibit 5-12.

Organization The organizational structure "bubble" contains three elements:

1. *The formal organizational structure*—the typical and traditional hierarchical organization chart that we often see when we look at a corporate profile.

2. *The informal organizational structure*—the way that work really gets done in organizations. In every organization we've encountered in the last twenty years, an organizational work-around exists between the formal organizational structure and the way work actually gets done. In fact, there exists an entire science of how to identify and map these alternate informal organizational structures. Informal organizational structures arise for many reasons, such as working around value-inhibiting rules, working around value-inhibiting managers such as Gus and Joe, and compensating for dysfunctional organizational designs.

Interestingly, union members can often effectively express their displeasure with management by conducting a "rule-book work slowdown." In these cases, the informal organization has had to compensate for so much value-inhibiting formal design that workers can punish management simply by following the formal rules to the letter—surely an irony unintended by the original framers of the formal design.

Clearly, organizational design teams should discern and understand the informal organization, because in any redesign effort, it will be essential to capture the speed, productivity, and camaraderie engendered by such an informal organizational design while seeking to overcome the dysfunctions that necessitated it.

"So much of what we call management consists in making it difficult for people to work."

—PETER F. DRUCKER, MANAGEMENT THINKER AND AUTHOR

3. *Management—the third element of organization in the congruence diagram.* Management is about preserving status quo, about control, about getting the value delivered, about getting the value out. Good management is critical for successful organizational performance, and most investors consider solid management as one of their key criteria in deciding whether to invest in a company. But too much management can stifle an organization and impede value delivery. Management design involves decisions on the levels, style, and amount of management in an organization.

In designing or redesigning the organization for optimal value criteria, it is essential to select elements of the formal and informal organization and of management design that are best aligned with the strengths, assets, and measures that drive the organization engine.

Process The process bubble contains work, workflow, equipment, technology, space, work-rules, and information—all of the nonpersonnel elements of the congruence diagram. It is essential in developing decisions in designing the organization. In effect, the reengineering movement looked at the world from the perspective of this bubble. Reengineering changed processes, and then processes forced changes in organization, culture, and people. That's an effective approach when all of the value resides in process change; however, for our purposes here, the size of the prize is much larger than process change.

We are looking here at decisions about the work with respect to its optimal alignment with the organization, culture, and people: in other words, the optimal alignment of work within the congruence diagram. Outside the congruence diagram, we're looking at the work's optimal alignment with business strategy, asset portfolios, and financial measures and structure. The process bubble is not an end in itself, but a means to an end. What we seek is not simply to improve the performance of processes, but to optimize value.

People The people bubble of the diagram encompasses recruiting, retaining, training, compensating, and incentivizing people. Decisions on whom we look to attract, to an organization, how we develop them, what behaviors we ask for, how we reward them, must all be internally consistent with strategic decisions in workflow, organizational design, and culture.

Culture The culture bubble—perhaps the most problematic and powerful element—has three major levers: decision making, values, and leadership. How these levers are set help determine the success of any organizational design—and they each have a wide variety of settings.

1. *Decision Making:* The most powerful way to change an organization's culture is to change the way decisions are made. The settings for this lever are powerful and telling:

- Centralized versus decentralized decisions
- "Gut" versus quality-processed decisions
- Management-made versus employee-made decisions

Changes in the decision lever have immediate and lasting consequences in cultural change. For example, a retail organization that decided overnight to allow every employee to individually and personally decide on refunding or rebating money for damaged product up to fifty dollars underwent a profound change from a hierarchical and directed culture to a collegial and collaborative one.

A professional services firm eliminated the detailed management review of expense reports on projects and found that employees would immediately take on more responsibility and accountability for their expenditures, ultimately resulting in lower across-the-board costs. Without a doubt, changing the way decisions are made remains the most powerful lever of cultural change in organizational design.

2. *Values.* The promulgation of values in organizations is either policy-based or principle-based. *Policy-based organizations* shape their culture through a detailed manual that attempts to anticipate every possible situation that an employee might encounter and supply answers for each one. Almost all older, large corporations are policy based, varying only by degree. In these companies, all employees are given a large book of corporate policies, which has grown over time, and employees are judged by the way they adhere to and comply with these policies.

Principle-based organizations try to hire individuals who share a certain set of values; then the company seeks to instill in those individuals a set of principles for guiding their behavior. There are few or no policies. Employees are judged by their willingness and ability to operate within that value system. Hybrids of these approaches to values also exist. But any radical change, whether it's from a policy-based to a principle-based organization or the other way around, profoundly affects culture.

"Leadership is the art of getting someone else to do something you want done because he wants to do it."

—DWIGHT D. EISENHOWER, U.S. PRESIDENT

3. *Leadership*. The third lever of cultural change, leadership, concerns bringing about change, pushing the envelope, going in new directions, breaking the glass. It is very much the opposite competency of management—which, as we saw in the organizational bubble, concerns having control, maintaining the status quo, getting the value delivered. Yet leadership and management are like having right and left hands; most people have both, but one hand is dominant. Individuals tend to be more comfortable in one or the other of the two roles. Some people can both manage and lead, but one of those abilities usually comes to them more naturally than the other.

In the United States, most organizations are over-managed and under-led. Leadership is not only a scarcer resource than management, but also most companies tend to subordinate leadership to good management. The third lever of cultural change, then, is how leadership is treated in organizations. Does an organization attempt to grow leadership, reward it, and put leaders in positions of authority and responsibility? Or does it treat leaders the way the U.S. Navy treated William Sims, the young gunnery officer who was considered an irritant and almost driven from the organization, saved only by the intervention of the President of the United States?

The four bubbles for the congruence diagram—organization, process, people, culture—encompass all the relevant questions about the key components of organizational design. Using the congruence diagram, we can further analyze and explore the descriptive vision that emerged from the Align step of our organizational redesign.

An optimized organizational design will not only align each of the components within the congruence diagram, but also will align the congruence diagram itself as the representation of the organizational and operational interdependent component of enterprise value—with the other three interdependent components (strategy; portfolio; finance). And the congruence diagram helps generate the next essential tool in organizational design: the decision table.

Decision Tables

The decision table seen in Exhibit 5-13 is used to identify the key decisions that need to be made and the options that we have within each decision. It helps us select an internally consistent set of choices if we are to take a systems view of the decisions we're going to make.

In the table, under organizational design, the column heads, which represent the decisions we're going to make, issue from a combination of three things we've looked at before:

Design Alternative	Staging & Level of Investment	Cultural Req's.	Sales Org.	Strategic Marketing	Marketing Org.	Clinical Org.	Regulatory Org.	Marketing Processes	People
Full Corp.	Fast, complete buildup	Base-line and tailor	In-house CSO	U.S. Center of Excellence	Product Teams	U.S. Center of Excellence	U.S. Center of Excellence	Base-line and tailor	Generalist/ Entrepren'rs Specialists
Virtual Full Corp.	Fast, partial buildup (heavily outsourced)	Specified common plus " clean sheet"	Some combination of the above . . .	Centralized in Europe	Therapeutic Area Team	Centralized in Europe	Centralized in Europe	Specified common plus " clean sheet"	Hybrid
Sales & Marketing Org. Only	Staged, complete buildup			Hybrid	Hybrid	Hybrid	Hybrid		
	Staged, partial buildup (heavily outsourced)	Clean sheet (Start-up?)						Clean sheet	

Key Near-Term U.S. Decisions

Exhibit 5-13 – Decision table.

- The center portion of the decision hierarchy diagram, which focused on the decisions we need to make in this organizational effort
- The vision of the optimized end state, which describes the organization we would like to build for the future
- The congruence diagram, which specified the considerations of organization, work, people, and culture that we need to consider in any organizational design we create

The column headings in Exhibit 5-13 represent the major decisions issuing from our organizational design work at this point. The options in each column come from both the discussion of the possibilities for the organizational future as we understand them, but especially benefit from the targeted benchmarking work we initiated in the Align step. Recall that we selected targeted benchmarking candidates based on the value of organizational design elements that could be found in analogous situations both within our industry and outside.

We used the work developed from that point forward to populate the decision tables with a rich and interesting set of choices within each decision column. But the real power of a decision table lies not in simply specifying the individual decision choices as separate and independent decisions, but rather in helping to develop a system of consistent, integrated, interrelated, interdependent decisions.

Each set of decisions will be seen as a pathway through the decision table. There are at least three pathways that we always like to examine in such a decision table:

1. *Momentum:* The momentum pathway describes the open "as is" pathway through the table—the route we are likely to take if nothing changes. This is also referred to as "Current Course and Speed." Understanding this pathway helps us agree on the vision of where we are, about which, as we saw earlier, there is often widespread disagreement. (Never underestimate the importance of understanding where you are. In any trip to a National Park, you must first understand the location of "you are here" on the map before you can get to any other destination.)

2. *An Aggressive Stretch Alternative:* It's useful to follow the look at the momentum pathway with a look at an aggressive alternative. Assume that in pursuing the alternative there are no constraints of money or competing priorities. This allows us to consider how we would reach our idealized vision with a set of organizational design choices if we could do what we want, when we want, and how we want.

3. *Low-Cost Alternative:* Looking at an organization design predicated on a low-cost alternative forces us to think of things such as outsourcing, keeping fixed costs variable through contract labor, sourcing to other parties, partnering, alliances, supply chain simplification, and much more.

Beginning with these three pathways—momentum, aggressive alternative, and low-cost alternative—it is useful then to develop other practical or desirable hybrids. Each should be a consistent, complete, comprehensive, and clear set of choices representing a pathway through the decision table. Organizations usually develop somewhere between a half dozen and a dozen organizational alternatives for the decision table. All of these alternatives must be evaluated, which brings us to the tools for doing so.

Qualitative and Quantitative Tools

Exhibit 5-14 shows how these decision alternatives can be screened based on several value measures and how tradeoffs will be highlighted. Financial screening measures, beyond net present value (NPV) of discounted cash flows and economic value added (EVA), can include:

- Cost versus benefits
- Variable versus fixed costs
- One-time versus ongoing costs
- Capital versus expense

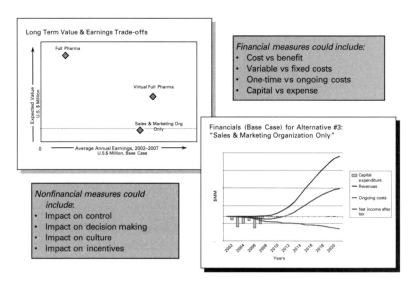

Exhibit 5-14 – Alternatives will be screened on several value measures, and trade-offs will be highlighted.

Nonfinancial measures could include:

■ Impact on control
■ Impact on decision making
■ Impact on culture
■ Impact on incentives

Selecting the right mix of qualitative and quantitative criteria, and their relative weight, is very much a function of what is wanted and needed from the organizational design.

Remember that the intent of the Define step is to select, on a systems level, the best possible definition of the organizational design system that will deliver optimal value for the enterprise. The deliverables of the Define step are shown in Exhibit 5-15.

On the basis of the Define step and the analysis, discussions, and decisions made, we produce a clear definition of what it is that we intend to design. We've not yet made all of the choices of specific details of the organizational design, but we have made specific decisions that are essential to that design. And those decisions have been made on the basis of the alignment to the larger value system, as well as to a specific understanding of the correlation to value. The organizational elements have not been selected in a void—arbitrarily or on the basis of political squabbling—but on the value of their contribution to the value of the implementation of the strategy.

- Most of the fundamental questions regarding the organization will be answered in this step, including rough estimates of timing and sizing
- Questions answered here include:
  —How to stage the build-up of the U.S. organization
  —Rough estimates on size of the organization over time
  —Identification of what work needs to be done by this organization as an operating unit and rough estimates on amount of work
  —Identification of the functions that must reside in the organization
  —Identification of what information will be needed and what information systems will be required to support the operating unit
  —Identification of the cultural requirements desired for the organization and in relationship to Corporate
  —Identification of what are desirable characteristics of the governance model
- Fast-track implementation activities and quick-win opportunities will be identified during this step
- Qualitative or quantitative trade-off analyses will be performed on any organizational requirements whenever it is not obvious what the best option is
- The corporate analysis will be completed and documented
- Teaming needs will be identified
- All of this will be documented in presentation formats or Word documents

Exhibit 5-15 – Define step deliverables.

Step Three: Design

"Luck is the residue of design."

—BRANCH RICKEY, FORMER OWNER OF THE BROOKLYN DODGER BASEBALL TEAM

The Design step builds on the Align and Define work. In the Align step, we developed a clear and coherent description of an ideal state three to five years in the future, a description aligned with the other interdependent elements of value. In the Define step, we developed the definition of several attractive organizational design requirements and from these, based on both qualitative and quantitative analysis and on what the enterprise both wants and needs, we selected the optimal set of defined requirements.

In step three we actually select the organizational design elements that best fit those defined requirements. This takes place in two stages:

1. *Architectural Design:* The first stage is a high-level systems design, analogous to designing the entire system in systems engineering. At this level, we want to design how all of the interdependent parts will work, but we will not make the deep dive into the specific selection of each of those interdependent parts.

2. *Detailed Design:* Here we take the plunge into making the detailed selection of each design element, specifying the specific item, system, job, or person who will best satisfy that design element. In systems engineering terms, this is akin to doing the deep dive into the individual components that make up the system. To extend the analogy, consider the move from an engineering bill of materials to a manufacturing bill of materials in systems design work. The engineering bill of materials, like the architectural design, defines the functional requirements necessary for each component of the system in order to make it work optimally. The manufacturing bill of materials, like the deep dive into components in the detailed design, specifies the specific named subsystem or part that will deliver the functionality called for and required by the engineering bill of materials.

We perform the Design step in these two stages in order to break down a complicated and sometimes seemingly insurmountable problem into discrete modules that we can address effectively. By first getting the system functions right, we can then attend to the specifics of the detailed selection of design components.

In both the architectural design stage and the subsequent detailed design stage, we can borrow generously from the work done in the targeted benchmarking. Targeted benchmarking was undertaken to provide us specific insights into a value-based catalog of organizational design elements that we could select. At the Design step, especially in the detailed design, elements of the organizational design identified in the targeted benchmarking often prove useful in the final design.

The deliverables from the Design step, as presented in Exhibits 5-16 and 5-17, include the answers to specific questions about the organizational levers in the congruence diagram covered earlier: organization, processes, people, and culture. To help answer these questions, it's useful to reintroduce a spider diagram— similar to the one we introduced for decision quality in Chapter 2—which shows the simultaneous and systematic development of integrated and interdependent elements of the value system (Exhibit 5-18). Instead of looking at organization, process, people, and culture as sequential events, we must look at their systematic and concurrent development.

As Exhibit 5-18 shows, value can be thought of as growing from point 0 on the inner circle to a point of 100 percent on the

- This step translates the organizational requirements into a high-level design of the organization.
- All of the work identified for the operating unit will be assigned to specific business processes.
- All business processes will be assigned to U.S. organization functions (marketing, sales, HR, etc.)
- The information requirements will be allocated across the business functions and business processes
- Information system alternatives will identified
- Decision authority for key strategic and operational decisions will be specified
- Facility requirements will be finalized
- Roles and job titles will be specified with estimates on head counts —High level job descriptions will be specified
- A description of the desired culture will be developed
- A preliminary design of governance processes will be specified
- A preliminary design of the organization structure will be specified
- Recruitment needs and a recruitment strategy will be constructed
- The roles of partners and teaming will be specified
- Fast-track implementation activities and quick wins will begin implementation
- All of this will be documented in presentation formats or Word documents

Exhibit 5-16 – Architectural organizational design deliverables.

outer circle, insofar as all of the interdependent elements of the system grow systematically and concurrently. The potential of the organizational design to grow in value from 0 to 100 percent depends upon its satisfying the requirements for the other elements of process, people, and culture. All of the elements must be in synch and aligned to produce that interdependent synergy.

So as we look at the questions that are answered by organizational design (shown in the exhibits), we need to explicitly understand that:

- This step creates a detailed design of the U.S. organization
- Information systems will be selected
- Facility layout plans will be completed
- All business processes will have detailed designs including
  —Work flow
  —Information flow
  —System usage
  —Roles and responsibilities
- Roles and job titles will be specified in detail with head counts specified
  —Detailed job descriptions will be completed
  —Training needs will be specified
- A detailed description of the desired culture will be finalized
- Detailed design of governance processes will be completed
- Detailed design of the organization structure will be completed
- Recruitment needs and plan will be documented and recruiting will be underway
- The specific roles of partners and teaming will be completed
- HR will be completely designed
- Fast-track implementation activities and quick wins will be fully underway
- All of this will be documented in presentation formats or Word documents

Exhibit 5-17 – Detailed organizational design deliverables.

■ The work must be designed to optimize the implementation of the strategy in the most efficient and effective manner, with full and complete attention to the organizational structure emerging, its culture, and its people.

■ The organizational levers—the formal organizational structure, the informal organizational structure, and the management structure—must be designed to optimize the work process.

■ The people of the organization must be selected, motivated, incentivized, compensated, trained, and retained in order to optimally perform the work of value delivery contained in the most practical and flexible organizational structure and culture.

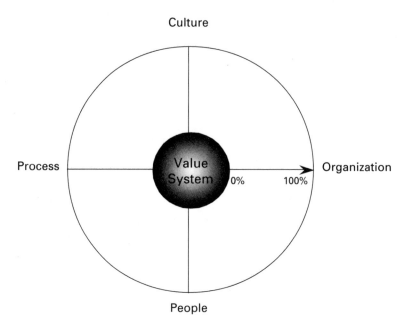

Exhibit 5-18 – A "spider" for congruence.

■ The culture of the organization and its associated levers of decision making, values promulgation, and leadership must be designed to optimize the organization and its people in the most productive and optimal completion of the work.

At the end of the Design step, we prepare a high-level implementation plan. This high-level plan outlines in broad strokes the final two steps of the organizational design process: *Commit* and *Build*.

Step Four: Commit

This step transforms the high-level implementation plan into three discrete planning documents:

1. A detailed implementation plan that includes milestones, responsibilities, and resource requirements on a detailed work-task breakdown. This requires good and deep project management.

2. A stakeholder communication plan that builds on the communications that have been going on throughout the organizational design project. However, this plan focuses explicitly on how all parties who will be influenced in any way by the organizational design need to be addressed:

- Their stake in the project
- The level of information they require
- The frequency of information
- The timing of information
- The form of the communication
- The legal or regulatory issues surrounding that communication
- The confidentiality of the communication
- The accuracy and truthfulness of the communication

3. An organizational alignment plan, which has two key components:

- One, when a subordinate part of a large organization has been designed or redesigned, it is essential to plan explicitly and in depth the alignment of the part to the whole and to manage that alignment during the building process.
- Two, it is essential in a major organizational design or redesign of all or part of an organization to have an ongoing alignment activity planned, because over time the forces of change tend to force the best of organizational design into misalignment. It is important to understand that eventual-

ity and to build in the ability to manage it and realign the organization as necessary.

Step Five: Build

Building the organization means executing the implementation plan. It requires the kind of solid program and project management discussed earlier. The humbling thought is that most of the failures in organizational design are blamed on this step, principally because they show up only at this step.

In studies conducted with thousands of senior executives about the failures of organizations following mergers and acquisitions, the executives responded as follows:

■ Approximately 30 percent attributed the failure to flawed strategy.

■ Almost 20 percent attributed failure to the negotiating of a bad deal that required earnings beyond those actually deliverable by the combined entity.

■ The most telling figure is that over 50 percent of the executives attributed the failure to the organizational design put into place following the merger. The interesting point is that the failure was perceived as one of organizational design because it showed up and was realized in organizational design. That is, in essence, the major lesson of this chapter and of this book.

We are designing a system of value. The system has interdependent parts. Organizational design—the engine of value delivery—can only be optimized when it is aligned and synchronized with the other three interdependent components: business strategy, asset portfolios, and financial measures and structure. If any of these components are weak, then the value chain will break and value will be lost.

CASE STUDY

Alpha Forest Products and Organizational Design

AFP was embarking on a bold course: moving from low-margin commodities to higher-margin, higher-value products, changing from an operations-focused organization to a market- and customer-facing company, divesting assets instead of acquiring them, and moving from unintegrated performance measures to an overriding, company-wide financial measure. The management team knew that all of this required revolutionary changes in its organization and operations.

After all, operations and organization are not only the agent of value delivery, but they are also the physical and actual manifestation of business strategy, asset portfolios, and financial measures and structure. For AFP, that meant changes for the organization itself, the work that was done, the people, and the culture. All of these levers of value would have to be reset in the new organizational and operational scheme of things.

The changes, once implemented, would be extraordinary:

- Marketing, not manufacturing, would determine what was built in the factories. Enormously expensive capital equipment would no longer run 24/7, but perhaps a mere half of that time, so that the machines could be cleaned and reconfigured in order to make different products on the same day.
- Long run-times to make a great deal of the same product would give way to short run-times to make numerous spot-market products.

- Price, and therefore profitability, would no longer be based exclusively on the product but on services that would be added to the mix, including:

  - Outsourcing

  - Contingency buying

  - Ensuring product availability throughout the cycle

  - Ensuring price throughout the cycle

  - Providing logistics and management services

Organizationally, these changes constituted a new market-leadership paradigm. In operations, they meant changing work rules that had been around for five generations. All of this would require explanation, training, retooling, reworking processes, and rethinking incentives.

AFP undertook a significant change management program throughout the entire organization. The goal: to align the organization, the work, the individuals, and the culture—the organization/operations component of value—with the other three interdependent components of value. The change programs at the operating level were extraordinarily successful. The unionized employees—who constituted over 70 percent of the total workforce—voted on numerous occasions (and against the advice of their leadership) to participate fully in the new ways of working. These workers saw clearly that the changes would produce value—from which they would benefit. They also saw that their leadership's objections were often rooted in long-standing feuds with the local management team rather than in real objections to the proposed changes. One factory quadrupled its profitability in the first twelve months. A second factory that should never have been EVA-positive has been EVA-positive ever since. And so it goes at AFP, where managing value as a system is now a way of life.

The Final Frontier

CHAPTER SIX

"Where there is an open mind, there will always be a frontier."

—CHARLES F. KETTERING, PRESIDENT, GENERAL MOTORS RESEARCH CORP. AND COFOUNDER, SLOAN-KETTERING INSTITUTE FOR CANCER RESEARCH

Going Where No Corporation Has Gone Before

In two separate surveys of 500 senior executives across multiple industries, respondents on average reported that their corporations capture only 60 percent of the potential value of their corporations, leaving a 40 percent performance gap. Independently and strikingly, these same senior executives reported that by perfectly aligning the corporation's business strategy, asset portfolios, financial measures and structure, and organization and operations, they could capture an additional 40 percent in value. In our many years of corporate experience we have never met any executives who believed that their organization had reached its ultimate performance level. In fact, the universal perspective has been that there is room for significant improvement regardless of which performance measure is being discussed.

Optimal alignment across the four components of the value system is of course an *ideal state*. No organization or corporation has reached it. Some, including General Electric, have made runs at this ideal state. But, as history shows and the media is quick to uncover, even those financial powerhouses have fallen short of such performance. But by being clear on what it would take to achieve such an optimal state of financial performance, we want to give leaders of organizations a path to follow—a map to break-through performance that enables repositioning of their organization on an improved efficient frontier, with a constant eye on something even better: the optimal efficient frontier of performance, the final frontier. From the perspective of efficient frontiers, Exhibit 6-1 identifies the path an organization would take to reach ever higher levels of performance.

We challenge business leaders and consultants alike to push toward this final frontier of corporate performance. How to get there is the ultimate corporate enigma. In this chapter we will explore organizational capabilities that are required for pursuing

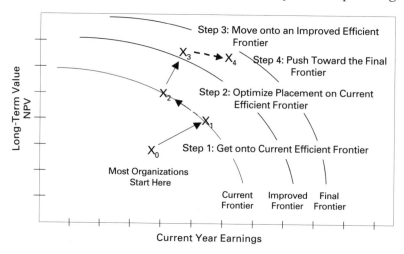

Exhibit 6-1 – An organization's path toward the optimal efficient frontier, the final frontier.

the final frontier. We do not have all of the answers, but we have discovered many of the paths that lead to that final frontier. We look forward to continuing the journey, and we challenge you to join us in the quest.

Making Strategic Decisions in the Context of a Network of Decisions

Central to the pursuit is the optimal alignment of the strategic decisions that are made throughout the organization. Earlier we discussed what you must account for when you make decisions and changes within each of the four components of the value system. Optimal financial performance can only be achieved if all of these decisions are aligned with respect to a preferred balance of short-term earnings and long-term shareholder value, obviously a Herculean feat. But using this yardstick as a measure will guide any organization to work towards aligning all strategic decisions to a common goal of corporate value creation. Exhibit 6-2 illustrates the classes of strategic decisions that span this network of decisions that must be aligned for optimal financial performance.

Beyond Risk Management to Risk Engineering

The topic of risk management is not new. Insurance companies have been honing their skills in it for three centuries. However, applying risk management successfully across the multitude of sources of risk in a business is both new and rare. While managing risk is a necessary corporate competency for sustainable growth in shareholder value, corporations can and should do much better. Value-maximizing corporations that *engineer* risk can ultimately redefine entire industries. Enron was on this path as it shed physical assets in exchange for information assets, and

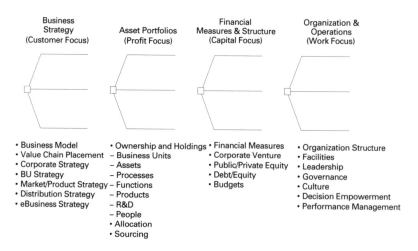

Business Strategy (Customer Focus)	Asset Portfolios (Profit Focus)	Financial Measures & Structure (Capital Focus)	Organization & Operations (Work Focus)
• Business Model	• Ownership and Holdings	• Financial Measures	• Organization Structure
• Value Chain Placement	– Business Units	• Corporate Venture	• Facilities
• Corporate Strategy	– Assets	• Public/Private Equity	• Leadership
• BU Strategy	– Processes	• Debt/Equity	• Governance
• Market/Product Strategy	– Functions	• Budgets	• Culture
• Distribution Strategy	– Products		• Decision Empowerment
• eBusiness Strategy	– R&D		• Performance Management
	– People		
	• Allocation		
	• Sourcing		

Exhibit 6-2 – Classes of decisions within the four components of the value system.

the company dominated energy trading until its accounting debacles all but destroyed it in the fall of 2001.

Exhibit 6-3 contrasts risk engineering with the kind of risk management that most organizations practice. Risk engineering extends the common approaches of risk management in two fundamental ways:

1. *Risk engineering focuses on minimizing the probability of a loss AND on maximizing the probability of a significant gain.* In practice, risk management focuses on minimizing the probability of a loss and pays little or no attention to upside or gain. Risk management rarely comes for free. It takes resources, both people and capital. When budgets tighten, risk management activities are often the first to be eliminated.

At most corporations, spending resources to protect against *uncertain* shortfalls or losses just doesn't seem to make the cut. Consequently, risk management, in practice, has more to do with identifying and resolving problems than with managing uncertainty. Not surprisingly, with little or no attention spent on the gain associated with uncertainty, risk management gets short shrift in many corporate settings.

2. Risk engineering uses an understanding of risk and uncertainty to determine the problem frame and decision space. In practice, risk management is applied to a given problem or situation. The problem or situation has a given frame, setting, and boundaries. Recall the acquisition of Hughes Electronics' defense business by Raytheon discussed in Chapter 2. Raytheon considered closing the Hughes west coast site and combining work forces in Raytheon's offices on the east coast. Typical risk management activities would identify the retention of key Hughes staff as a risk item and go about risk mitigation plans to re-recruit the key staff. The assumed givens in this situation include the acquisition and the closing of the Hughes site.

Risk engineering would identify the same risk—retention of key Hughes staff—but would use this information to influence the decision frame. Should the closing of the Hughes site be reconsidered? Depending on the magnitude of the key staff retention risk, the answer could be yes. You can't know until you measure the risk. The bottom line here is simple. We must use

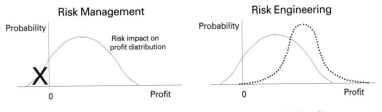

Exhibit 6-3 – Comparison of risk management to risk engineering.

our understanding of uncertainty and risk to help us frame our issues, problems, concerns, and ultimately, the decisions we make.

Capability Requirements for Pursuing the Final Frontier

To pursue alignment of the four components of the value system, organizations must have the following essential capabilities. (This is not a comprehensive list, since additional capabilities are needed to achieve alignment.) Organizations must be able to:

■ *Build decision quality into the decisions within and across the four components of the value system.* The concept of decision quality, defined in Chapter 2, offers a powerful means for pursuing the final frontier. In our experience, simply building decision quality into isolated strategic decisions in any of the four components of the value system results in at least 30 percent improvement in value creation. Often, it produces as much as 150 percent improvement over current courses of action. Aligning strategic decisions within and across the four components of the value system improves financial performance even more.

■ *Make an explicit commitment to shareholder value creation throughout the organization.* Most corporations pursue goals that are often conflicting. Following Jack Welch's philosophy of being number one or two in a market or getting out of it remains a common goal in corporate America. Unfortunately, being number one or number two in your market doesn't necessarily imply optimal value creation. Through the 1980s and into the early 1990s, Cadbury Schweppes explicitly and publicly attempted to catch Pepsi and Coke in volume and market share. Throughout this period of growth, Cadbury's stock price consistently lagged behind the market leaders, despite the consistent, favorable reputation Cadbury enjoyed. That all changed when

John Sunderland became CEO of Cadbury in 1996. Sunderland publicly promised investors that Cadbury would double its stock price every five years. As a result of the company's judicious acquisitions and organic growth, Cadbury's share price went from about ten dollars in 1995, prior to Sunderland's public commitment to shareholder value growth, to over thirty dollars by 1999.

Making an explicit, public commitment to growth in shareholder value produces at least two beneficial impacts: One, it puts the market on alert to expect major positive changes within the corporation, which attracts investor interest and appetite. Two, it creates the necessary sense of urgency within the corporation to catalyze the necessary changes. According to Haspeslagh, Noda, and Boulos,[1] explicitly committing to shareholder value increases the chances of significantly and positively affecting the stock price. Their studies suggest that companies that explicitly commit to shareholder value are more than twice as likely to positively influence stock price as those companies where the commitment is only implicit.

The caveat here is that in some parts of the world, such as Europe, the term "shareholder value" is considered politically incorrect by governments, unions, and even employees. Consequently, in those situations, the shareholder value perspective can be highly beneficial at the executive level but communicating that perspective is, at best, risky.

■ *Ensure that decisions and actions have an explicit traceable link to a shareholder value measure and a short-term profitability measure.* Recall that placement on an efficient frontier represents a decision that balances short-term cash needs and the long-term growth in shareholder value (see Exhibit 6-1 as well as the discussion on efficient frontiers in Chapter 3). Understanding how individuals' actions and decisions affect short-term profitability and long-term shareholder value makes it easy for employees to understand how they can best contribute to organizational goals and objectives.

In general, individuals want to contribute to corporate performance, but they are unclear on how best to do it, and they are besieged with mixed signals. Although you could envision a shareholder value model and profitability model that could calculate corporate contribution based on individual performance and decision making, that degree of complexity is not required. In most cases, if individuals understand directionally—that is, positive or negative—the contribution of their decisions and actions, their alignment to corporate performance greatly improves.

■ *Incorporate risk engineering to establish decision and problem-solving frames.* Before you establish decision frames or problem-solving frames, discussions should include the significant risks associated with the decision or problem. The understanding of the risk should then be used to reflect on the potential decision and problem frame to determine whether there is a better frame that enables you to beneficially reposition the significant risks. Thus, you can eliminate, hedge, or mitigate risks. Doing this well takes practice, but it is certainly a learnable skill. However, it takes discipline to build this into your thought processes, and it must be built into your organization's decision and issue resolution processes as well.

■ *Ensure that performance measurement systems are explicitly linked to a shareholder value measure, the primary financial measure.* As we know, you get what you measure. By explicitly linking the performance measurement system and its specific measures to a primary corporate performance metric such as shareholder value, you motivate individuals to generate what the corporation's owners want—shareholder value. To make the performance measurement system work well, you must strongly tie it to compensation through performance-based compensation.

■ *Ensure that individual incentives and compensation are aligned with the primary financial measure.* Haspeslagh, Noda, and Boulos[2] report that successful value-based management (VBM) programs almost always increase everyone's ownership stake in the company and, thereby, in the program. But they found that "the size of the compensation package was not a factor in determining success, only how wide the program was in its coverage." They report that 53 percent of the successful VBM programs use a widespread compensation program (greater than 50 percent of the employees participating), whereas 76 percent of the unsuccessful VBM programs lacked a widespread compensation program.

Siemens abandoned an executive compensation scheme that was based on a set of internal performance measures with little performance-related pay. Instead, the company now ties 60 percent of the compensation for the top 500 executives to performance. Executive compensation for any given year is based on the current share price and the incremental improvement in the EVA the investors expect for the year. If Siemens meets that EVA hurdle, then the executives are paid 100 percent of their targeted compensation. And if Siemens surpasses the EVA hurdle and hits some secondary targets, then the executives can double their target compensation. Other compensation programs are used for lower levels in Siemens, so that about 20 percent of all Siemens employees are compensated based on attaining EVA targets.

■ *Ensure that all strategic decisions comprehend and account for impacts across all four value system components.* As we saw in Chapters 2 through 5, perfect alignment across the four components of the value system requires that all strategic decisions in each of the value system components and across the components comprehend and account for impacts across the value system. Moreover, to truly comprehend, compare, and contrast those impacts, all of these decisions should use a common, primary value measure.

■ *Design the organization to be both adaptive and flexible.* Change is ubiquitous. Industries differ only in the rate of change with respect to technology, market demands, competitive actions, and political climate. Being adaptive and flexible as an organization is not a competitive advantage but a requirement to survive the next business cycle. Adaptability and flexibility apply both to the decisions and actions that reside in each of the four components of the value system and to the means used to execute the actions and make the decisions.

Pursuing the Final Frontier Requires a Cultural Transformation

For an organization to approach the final frontier of performance, the behaviors, decisions, and actions of every individual must be consistent and aligned with the creation of maximum shareholder value. Obviously, this amounts to the ultimate cultural transformation of an organization. Two important facets of a shareholder value focused cultural transformation include:

1. The underlying operating principles and characteristics of the transformation
2. The role of education and training

William Joyce[3] introduced the concept of "method-as-model." According to Joyce, the methods that are used to change organizations must themselves model the desired future state of the organization. Thus, changing an organization into a culture in which individuals exhibit behaviors, decisions, and actions that maximize shareholder value creation requires the executives and managers leading the change to exhibit those characteristics themselves. Moreover, the methods and characteristics employed throughout the change process should mirror the desired changes to be built into the work within and across the four components of the value system.

This is crucial from the outset of the transformation process. Otherwise, people become skeptical, and even cynical, when they are recruited into a change project by a leadership that espouses one set of principles and then employs those principles inconsistently in the pursuit of the desired changes. The change methodology itself should be the first, observable incarnation of the change sought. Exhibit 6-4 contrasts the characteristics of a typical organization to the characteristics of a shareholder–value-focused organization. The desirable characteristics of the future organization, listed in Exhibit 6-4, should be built into the transformation process itself.

Current Culture	Value-Focused Culture
• Many diverse approaches	• Consistent language and approaches
• Volume orientation	• Value orientation
• Measuring value only	• Measuring value and risk
• Close to the chest —Distrust —Solo	• Open collaboration and idea sharing
• Information assembled to defend	• Information to guide inquiry
• Single alternative developed	• Multiple alternatives proactively considered
• Avoidance of attribution for fear of retribution	• Attribution encouraged to facilitate open discussion
• Errors of omission (opportunity cost) are minor, errors of commission (poor results) are huge	• Errors of omission and commission are equally viewed as detracting from value
• Advocacy frame —"Winning = approval"	• Learning and advocacy frames 1) Strong inquiry and knowledge sharing 2) "Winning = quality decisions"
• Senior decision makers "making the call"	• Senior decision makers focus on how to enhance value in the process

Exhibit 6-4 – The characteristics of a shareholder-value-focused cultural transformation.

Haspeslagh, Noda, and Boulos[4] report the critical importance of training for value–based-management (VBM) programs and say that "getting VBM right demands that everyone in the company be convinced that managing for value is the right thing to do." Their research shows that successful VBM companies invest "a great deal of time, effort, and money in training large numbers of their employees." They report that 62 percent of the successful VBM companies train over 75 percent of their managers in VBM concepts, whereas only 27 percent of the unsuccessful companies trained that large a proportion of management.

The obvious correlation in management training to the success of VBM programs can be extended to the successful implementation of the vision presented in this book, a vision that transcends VBM programs. Providing sufficient training to management prior to the enrollment of management in the pursuit of the final frontier is a must. The training required encompasses the characteristics of the value-focused culture detailed in Exhibit 6-4.

CASE STUDY

Alpha Forest Products and the Enigma of Corporate Value

Alpha Forest Products now manages value as a single system, having transformed itself in precisely the ways we have been recommending here. AFP moved from a bottom-tier, low-performing company competing in its space to a high performing—and in the last year the highest performing—company competing in its space. How? By solving the enigma of corporate value.

We began this book with that deeply perplexing enigma: Why do senior executives in major corporations *knowingly* allow so much of the value potential to leak out of their organizations, to simply get away? Clearly, they understand the consequences of operating things as they do: They report a "value gap" of 40 percent; some 68 percent of respondents see their organizations as impeding value; and only 1 percent report managing the four interdependent components of value as a single, integrated system of value. Yet, in most cases, they simply fail to act.

Why don't senior executives do what they know they must? We suggested that the answer is two-fold: One, they lack the understanding to do it, and two, they lack the will. Those are formidable obstacles. AFP overcame both. As we saw, AFP's senior management team began with an open-minded, determined search for knowledge. In their high-inquiry mode, they built on the many lessons they had learned through various improvement programs over the years, and they sought to leverage those competencies and capabilities, which had been honed in the organization, to build the kind of integrated system of value we have described here in such detail. Then came the hard part: *doing it.*

And so came the exercise of will. For AFP, that meant a disciplined determination to shake off the heavy burden of the past. They had to overcome the legacy of a commodities-business mindset, organizational intractability, cultural avoidance of conflict and change, and the fact that the company appeared to be an "old business" permanently trapped in the "old economy." Through the combination of methodological know-how and the will of its leaders, AFP broke decisively with its past. They solved—or better yet—*resolved* the enigma of corporate value. They acquired the knowledge and summoned the will, and now they have pushed toward that final frontier described in this chapter.

It's an enviable success story. And in its end lies the beginning. Because for readers who have followed the story to this conclusion, the challenge ahead is how to get started. The next and final chapter provides some ideas and tools that can help you make that happen.

Notes

1. Philippe Haspeslagh, Tomo Noda, and Faers Boulos, "Managing for Value: It's Not Just About the Numbers," *Harvard Business Review,* July–August 2001, p. 67.
2. Ibid.
3. William F. Joyce, *Mega Change: How Today's Leading Companies Have Transformed Their Workforces* (New York: The Free Press, 1999), pp. 53–55.
4. Haspeslagh, Noda, and Boulos, "Managing for Value," p. 68.

Getting Started

CHAPTER SEVEN

"The value of an idea lies in the using of it."

—THOMAS A. EDISON, AMERICAN INVENTOR

Closing the Value Gap

As an executive, do you know what is the next set of strategic actions you should be taking, as an organization, to balance short-term earnings requirements with long-term shareholder value growth? Striking this critical balance is as simple as knowing what your focus should be and sticking to it. But knowing your focus and aligning your organization to this focus is no simple matter and requires a concerted effort. The resistance of executives to significant change is understandable. Many executives and organizations are caught in a cycle of lost opportunities (see Exhibit 7-1). This was certainly the case for Alpha Forest Products. AFP needed an event to jump-start the changes they needed.

We stated in Chapter 1 that executives don't do what they

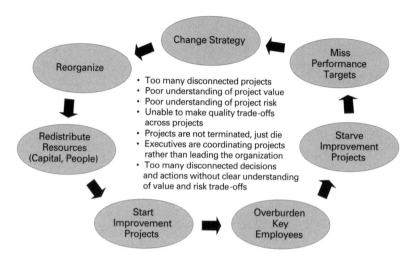

Exhibit 7-1 – The cycle of lost opportunities.

know they must do for the simple reason that they don't know how to do it. Not knowing the *how* saps the *will* to make an attempt. The previous chapters described much about how to close the 40 percent value gap. This chapter reveals proven, practical recipes for jump-starting a program to close the elusive value gap. We have found that executing a quick, jump-starting initiative that illuminates the path to closing the value gap creates the energy, expectations, and most importantly, the *will*. As the Italian expression goes, "with the eating comes the appetite."

A quick, systematic start creates the organizational appetite. We have learned time and time again that the key to a successful jump-start is speed. But before we delve into the details of how to execute a speedy jump-start; let's first try to understand the underlying framework of the system that we will be modifying as we pursue the closing of the value gap.

What Is an Organization's Value System?

Every organization has an underlying value system (Exhibit 7-2) that can be thought of as a system of four components:

1. Business strategy
2. Asset portfolios
3. Financial measures and structure
4. Organization and operations

Of utmost importance to the value system are the interrelationships and dependencies among and across the four components. Optimal value creation requires that each of these four components be aligned. Lack of alignment of even one of these four components will significantly inhibit the creation of value. Most organizations have competency and a natural tendency to focus on one or more of these components; but only the most successful organizations master strategic decision-making and change across all four.

The Thirty-Day Jump Start

A journey of 1,000 miles starts with one step. The first step towards closing the value gap is a thirty-day jump-start activity that will reveal the path forward. This chapter provides proven

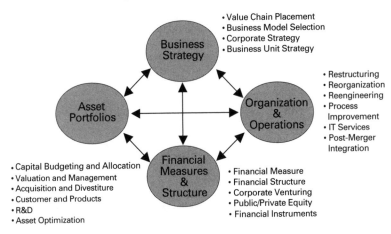

Exhibit 7-2 – The four components of an organization's value system and their corresponding levers.

recipes for successful jump-starts. To suggest that this is merely the first step of the journey is an understatement. The first thirty days will be a *leap*.

The thirty-day jump start consists of four weeks of activities, with each week focused on a specific theme and set of deliverables. The four weeks are:

Week 1: Launch the Jump Start
Week 2: Envision the Opportunities
Week 3: Align to the Program
Week 4: Plan the Program

The activities associated with the four weeks can easily be remembered using the acronym *LEAP* (Launch-Envision-Align-Plan).

Week 1: Launch the Jump Start

The first week of activity focuses on deciding a thematic scope, designing and staging the four weeks of work, creating the templates and tools, and scheduling the resources—people and facilities. We have found that senior executives typically desire having one of three primary or thematic focuses for a jump-start activity:

1. Revenue growth (top-line performance)
2. Operational effectiveness and efficiency (bottom-line performance)
3. Asset portfolio optimization

Throughout this chapter we provide examples of a revenue growth program to illustrate the work and deliverables of the jump-start activity.

Questions to Be Answered During "Launch" Phase

- What should be the primary, thematic focus of the program—revenue growth, operational effectiveness and efficiency, and/or asset portfolio optimization?

- Who should participate in the four-week activity and at what capacity?
- What skills or knowledge are not represented by participants, and how can we remedy these gaps?
- Do we need to perform targeted benchmarking on any of our strategic, value-adding processes? (Used for an Operational Effectiveness and Efficiency Program.)
- Do we need to perform targeted asset performance benchmarking for any of our assets? (Used for an Asset Portfolio Optimization Program.)
- What and how should we communicate this activity to key stakeholders (employees, corporate, suppliers, lenders, etc.)?
- What questions should we ask participants if we use a value gap diagnostic survey? How should we administer the survey (online/Web-based, telephone interview, in-person interview)?

Activities and Deliverables to Be Completed During "Launch" Phase

Activity L.1: *Decide on program focus/theme.*

Activity L.2: *Document jump-start plan* (schedule and resources).

Activity L.3: *Schedule resources* (people and facilities).

Activity L.4: *Design value gap diagnostic survey.* This activity includes specifying the questions and creating the delivery mechanism. Exhibit 7-3 provides an example of a diagnostic survey focused on determining the degree of alignment among managers and executives with respect to the business unit's strategy and the focus of the organization's strategy implementation.

Here are some additional example diagnostic questions for a revenue-growth–focused program:

Goal How will we measure success?	Growth	Low Cost/High Productivity	Asset Utilization

Strategy How does our market grow?	Emerging Growth Market	Stable Growth Market	Mature Market
When do we take the value out?	Create Long-Term Value	More Short-Term Value	Harvest Value
How can we lead in our market?	Product/Service Leader	Low Cost Leader	Customer Affinity Leader

Our Defining Strength or Competency: Raw Material | Supply Chain | Access to Innovation | Optimization Culture | Infrastructure Decisions | Capacity | Logistics | Information | Strong Culture | Value Added SVC Focus | Aligned w/ Customer | Access to Markets

Strategy Implementation What do customers value most?	Product/Service Attributes	Relationship Attributes	Image Attributes
How do we fill customer needs?	Innovation Processes	Operations Processes	CRM Processes
Where are we investing most?	Innovation Processes	Operations Processes	CRM Processes
What will help us learn and grow?	Staff Competencies	Technology	Climate for Change

Exhibit 7-3 – Example of a segment of a value gap diagnostic survey used to assess the degree of alignment among managers and executives with respect to the business unit's strategy and the focus of strategy implementation efforts.

- Which channel would produce the most shareholder value growth potential over the next three to five years: (a) traditional, non–Web-based, (b) Web-based, or (c) nontraditional, non–Web-based?
- From the perspective of risk versus return, which acquisition strategy represents the best approach to achieving the organization's three- to five-year goals: (a) acquisition of new verticals, (b) acquisition of new businesses, or (c) acquisition of add-ons?
- Which region has the greatest shareholder value potential for the organization: (a) Western Europe, (b) Asia/Pacific, (c) Central/South America, or (d) Middle East/Africa?
- From the perspective of risk versus return, which market/ product combination has the most shareholder value potential: (a) existing products/existing markets, (b) existing

products/new markets, (c) new products/existing markets, or (d) new products/new markets?

See Exhibit 7-4 for an example of a general list of value-gap diagnostic questions that span the four dimensions of the organization's value system. Exhibit 7-5 illustrates an assessment/diagnostic tool to support determining which components of the value system should receive the most attention and effort. To use this tool have each executive assess the degree of appropriateness/alignment of each of the four components of the value system, on a scale of 0 to 100 percent. Large variations in scores, or low scores for any one component, suggest that a discussion is required to determine whether action is required. This tool can be used during the jump-start activity and during the course of any subsequent program of activities focused on closing the value gap.

Activity L.5: *Design and create jump-start templates and tools.*

Business Strategy	Organization and Operations
• Should we consider our placement in the customer value chain and if so, what areas should we consider pursuing? • Should we consider redefining the customer value chain and redefining our industry and role and if so, how? • How much shareholder value are we leaving on the table with our current value chain placement? • What are the strategic business model decisions we need to make in the near-term?	• What change initiatives should we be pursuing, canceling, postponing, or reconsidering? • Do we have the right individuals leading our change initiatives? • Are our change initiatives sufficiently coordinated? • Do we need to improve the governance and communications within and across our change initiatives?
Asset Portfolios	**Financial Measures and Structure**

• Should we consider revisiting our:
  - business unit holdings and determine which to acquire or divest?
  - product and service offerings and determine which to continue offering, terminate, or pursue?
  - asset holdings and determine which to acquire or divest?
  - portfolio of R&D investments in terms of types and levels of investment?
  - business processes and functions and determine which to keep, which to outsource, and which to terminate?
• What are the strategic asset portfolio decisions we need to make in the near-term?
	• Do we need to restructure our debt to position ourselves better for our strategy and future business model?
	• Should we consider establishing an internal venture capital organization?
	• Do we need capital and, if so, what are the sources we should be considering?
	• What level of funding do we need to pursue the changes we need to make?
	• Do we need to overhaul our measurement systems to ensure they are aligned with the changes we need to pursue and with our incentive systems?

Exhibit 7-4 – Value gap diagnostic questions across the four dimensions of an organization's value system.

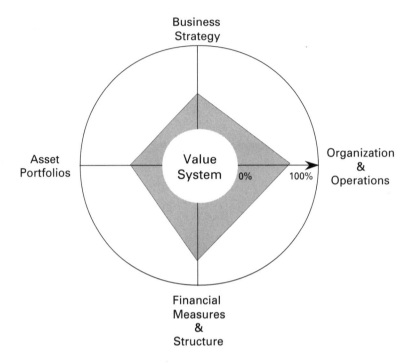

Exhibit 7-5 – Value system diagnostic tool for determining degree of completeness of work in each value system component.

For a revenue-growth–focused program during the jump-start activities or workshops, use a simple approach to focus multiple teams on different ways to generate additional revenue. As shown in Exhibit 7-6, a workshop could be designed around four teams working four different product/market segments. In this case we define an *existing product* as an existing revenue stream from a current product or service offering. A *new product* is a new revenue stream from a new product or service offering, or a combination of current offerings (hybrid). An *existing market* is made up of current targeted geographies and current customers, whereas a *new market* is made up of new geography targets or a new customer. Exhibits 7-7A, 7-7B, and 7-7C are sample templates used

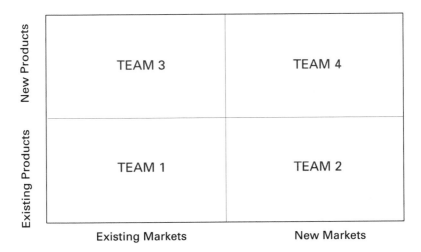

Exhibit 7-6 – Four separate teams focused on four separable market/ product segments.

for breakout groups focused on creating and prioritizing revenue growth ideas.

Activity L.6: *Design and communicate message from executive-in-charge.*

Week 2: Envision the Opportunities

The focus of the second week is on getting a sense of the magnitude of the value gap—the size of the prize, understanding the obstacles and constraints to closing the value gap, administering a value gap diagnostic to achieve an internal perspective, and performing any required research on markets and competition to gain a sufficient external perspective.

Questions to Be Answered During "Envision" Phase
■ What should be the target goals for the program? How aggressive can we make them without sacrificing realism? (Example: double revenue in five years.)

Title: _____

Description: _____

_____

Customer(s): _____

_____

Why is the idea compelling to the customer? Why would a customer pay for this? _____

_____

What is the preferred marketing/sales channel? _____

_____

_____

Competition: _____

_____

Investment Required: _____

_____

Given successful implementation, what is the range of revenue that this idea would generate in 2005? (as measured in millions of dollars):

Low Value-   (10th percentile): _____
Nominal Value- (50th percentile): _____
High Value-   (90th percentile): _____

Exhibit 7-7A – Template used for documenting revenue-generating ideas in a workshop breakout session.

- What are the obstacles, issues, challenges, and constraints that could keep us from reaching the target goals?
- What strategic, value-adding processes should be in focus? (Used for an Operational Effectiveness and Efficiency Program.)
- What assets should be in focus? (Used for an Asset Portfolio Optimization Program.)
- What relevant actions are our competitors taking?
- What relevant changes are taking place in our markets?

	Opportunity	Resources	Timing	Investment Range ($K)	2005 Revenue Range ($M)	Comments
1						
2						
3						
4						
5						
6						
7						
8						
9						
10						

Exhibit 7-7B – Template used for summarizing a *team's* revenue generating ideas in a workshop breakout session.

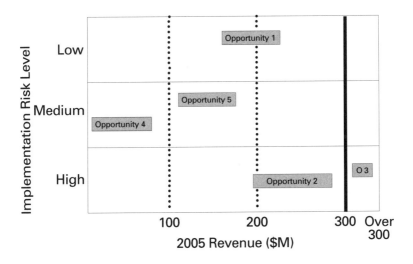

Exhibit 7-7C – Template used for communicating the risk versus revenue of team-generated opportunities in a workshop breakout session.

Activities and Deliverables to Be Completed During "Envision" Phase

Activity E.1: *Administer and interpret the value gap diagnostic.* As an example, Exhibit 7-8 displays the results of a segment of a value gap diagnostic survey illustrating the sources of misalignment within an organization with respect to overall strategy and strategy implementation.

Activity E.2: *Perform required benchmarking and information collection activities.*

Activity E.3: *Identify and document internal and external obstacles, issues, challenges, and constraints to achieving program target goals.*

Activity E.4: *Identify and document categories/classes of opportunities.* As an example of a revenue-growth–focused program, the growth themes could include:

Strategy			
How does our market grow?	Emerging Growth Market 2	Stable Growth Market 36 ★	Mature Market 10
When do we take the value out?	Create Long-Term Value 22 ◄-------►	More Short-Term Value 20 ★	Harvest Value 6
How can we lead in our market?	Product/Service Leader 24 ◄-------	Low Cost Leader 0 -------►	Customer Affinity Leader 24 ★
Our Defining Strength or Competency	Raw Material 4 / Supply Chain / Access to Innovation 2 / Optimization Culture 2	Infrastructure Decisions / Capacity / Logistics / Information 7	Strong Culture 10 ★ / Value Adding SVC Focus 4 / Aligned w/ Customer 6 / Access to Markets 15

Strategy Implementation			
How will we measure success?	Growth 42 ★	Low Cost/High Productivity 2	Asset Utilization 4
What do customers value most?	Product/Service Attributes 31 ◄-------	Relationship Attributes 8 ★ -------►	Image Attributes 8
How do we fill customer needs?	Innovation Processes 11 ★◄----	Operations Processes 17 -------►	CRM Processes 18
Where are we investing most?	Innovation Processes 12	Operations Processes 28 ★	CRM Processes 8
What will help us learn and grow?	Staff Competencies 29 ★	Technology 2	Climate for Change 17

★ Executive-in-Charge

Exhibit 7-8 – Example of a segment of a value gap diagnostic with the results of the survey. (Numbers indicate how many respondents answered the question with the specific answer.)

- Grow by sweetening our deals.
- Use customer information to grow share of wallet.
- Target high revenue customers.
- Acquire online businesses.
- Publish real time data products.

Week 3: Align to the Program

During the third week, the work consists of creating the specific opportunities, assessing the magnitudes of their value contribution, assessing the risk in pursuing the specific opportunities, prioritizing the opportunities, estimating the resources and timing of the opportunities, and ultimately aligning the senior executive team to a prioritized list of opportunities.

Questions to Be Answered During "Align" Phase

- What are the specific opportunities to be considered?
- What is the list of potential opportunities we could pursue?
- What are the benefits, costs, and risks associated with each opportunity?
- Which opportunities can be classified as "quick wins"? (Completed within the next ninety days)
- Which opportunities require strategic decisions to be made?
- Which opportunities can proceed straight into a change project and require no strategic decisions to be made?
- What is the prioritized list of opportunities?
- Which opportunities should we pursue this quarter, this year, and within three years?

Exhibit 7-9 illustrates the overall flow of a workshop focused on answering the above questions. For the example of the revenue-growth–focused program with four separate teams split

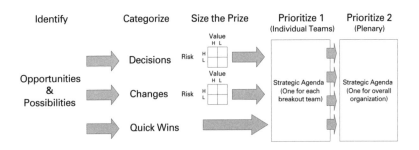

Exhibit 7-9 – Example of the flow of workshop activities, starting with a broad list of opportunities culminating in a strategic agenda for the overall organization.

by markets and products, each team creates and prioritizes a list of potential opportunities using a template such as depicted in Exhibit 7-7B.

Activities and Deliverables to Be Completed During "Align" Phase

Activity A.1: *Identify and document a list of potential opportunities.* Exhibit 7-7A details the level of detail that is sufficient for this exercise for a revenue-growth–focused program.

Activity A.2: *Assess the relative risk for each potential opportunity*: Using a high-, medium-, and low-risk approach is sufficient for this activity.

Activity A.3: *Map the potential opportunities on a risk versus benefit basis.* Exhibit 7-7C provides an example of the results of doing this exercise.

Activity A.4: *Prioritize the list of opportunities.* For the revenue growth example, have each of the four teams prioritize their list of opportunities and subsequently create a final prioritized list accounting for the entire set of potential opportunities across all four teams. More specifically, have each of the four teams create thirty potential opportunities and then have each of the four teams identify their "top ten" opportunities. Have all of the members of the four teams meet in a plenary session to review the four "top ten" lists and determine the final list of prioritized opportunities to be pursued by the organization—the *draft strategic agenda*. This list of opportunities to be pursued by the organization will be scrubbed and organized during the last week of the jump-start activity focused on planning.

Note on prioritization: We have found that prioritization of opportunities through voting is a quick and efficient means to identify the opportunities that the executive team truly has sufficient confidence in and will commit to. Exhibit 7-10 presents an example scoring format for prioritizing processes to be redesigned under an overall program focused on operational effectiveness and efficiency.

Week 4: Plan the Program

The draft strategic agenda resulting from the previous week's effort needs to be organized and structured into a program format.

KEY
0 = No Impact
10 = Maximum Impact

	GOALS				RESOURCES		FACTORS				
Process	Regain Market Share	Capture 70% Share	Maintain Gross Profit	ROI 20%	FTE	$	Time	Cost	Risk	Social	Priority
Develop Product	0	8	5	5	15	2,500,000	Med.	$$	High	Easy	3
Manufacture	0	9	7	7	375	29,300,000	Long	$$$$	Med.	Hard	2
Fulfill Orders	8	9	9	9	22.5	2,500,000	Med.	$$	Med.	Med.	1a
Service Customer Request	6	8	5	5	9	700,000	Short	$	Low	Easy	1b
Maintain Customer Accounts	3	3	3	3	8.5	1,000,000	Short	$	Low	Easy	
Develop Human Resources	4	6	4	4	6.5	765,000	Long	$	Med.	Hard	
Compensate	3	5	3	3	11.5	1,350,000	Med.	$	High	Hard	
Fund	3	3	3	3	9	1,060,000	Med.	$	Med.	Easy	
Comply	1	1	1	1	7	825,000	Med.	$	Med.	Med.	
Acquire Customer Orders	7	7	8	8	36	5,000,000	Med.	$$$	High	Med.	1c

Exhibit 7-10 – Example of a scoring/prioritization system for processes used in an operational effectiveness- and efficiency-focused program.

At this point in the process, you will have a team of individuals—senior executives, executives, and managers—aligned to a list of opportunities and actions. This is a critical point. *The critical players are aligned to the listed opportunities because they were the ones who identified the opportunities and prioritized them.* Inevitably, there will be some overlap and obvious linkages among the activities in the draft strategic agenda. Consequently some bundling and grouping of the listed opportunities will have to be performed.

Additionally, the list of opportunities needs to be partitioned into three categories: decision-focused initiatives, change-focused initiatives, and quick wins. The importance of making the distinction between initiatives that require making strategic decisions—decision-focused initiatives—and initiatives that can proceed straight into change/implementation activities—change focused initiatives—is that they require distinctly different forms of leadership and different project approaches. Individuals leading decision-focused initiatives should naturally be inclined to the characteristics of *thought leadership*. On the other hand, individuals leading change-focused initiatives should naturally be inclined to the characteristics of *change leadership* (refer to Exhibit 2-4 in Chapter 2). Decision-focused projects require a project approach that builds decision quality into the process. Refer to Chapter 2 for the definition of decision quality.

Questions to Be Answered During "Plan" Phase
- What are the initiatives on the organization's strategic agenda?
- Which initiatives are classified as quick wins, which should be completed this year, and which should be completed within three years?
- Who is responsible for successfully completing each initiative?

- What resources are required for each initiative? (People, capital, and expenses) What is the governance structure for the overall program? (leadership team membership, issue resolution and critical decision-making process, organizational alignment activities, communications.)
- What is the overall timeline for completing this program of initiatives?

Activities and Deliverables to Be Completed During "Plan" Phase

Activity P.1: *Bundle and group initiatives appropriately from the draft strategic agenda.*

Activity P.2: *Classify initiatives as "decision focused," "change focused," or "quick wins."*

Activity P.3: *Identify leaders for each initiative.* Remember to consider the differences in thought leadership required for decision-focused initiatives and change leadership for change-focused initiatives.

Activity P.4: *Resource and schedule each initiative.*

Activity P.5: *Establish the leadership team and governance structure/processes.*

Activity P.6: *Align leadership team to program.* The leadership team must be fully aligned to the program content, target goals and objectives, resource requirements, schedule, governance structure and processes, and their role in achieving a successful program. Consequently, a final meeting should be held to achieve the go-forward "hand-shake" with the leadership team.

Exhibit 7-11 provides a summary and checklist for executing a LEAP jump-start activity.

Summary

The key principles of the book are best illustrated by looking at our business-to-business company, Alpha Forest Products, and

		Percentage Completion				
		0%	25%	50%	75%	100%
Launch the Jump Start	L.1- Decide on Program Focus/Theme					
	L.2- Document Jump-Start Plan (Schedule and Resources)					
	L.3- Schedule Resources (People and Facilities)					
	L.4- Design Value Gap Diagnostic Survey					
Envision the Opportunities	E.1- Administer and Interpret the Value Gap Diagnostic					
	E.2- Perform Required Benchmarking and Information Collection Activities					
	E.3- Identify and Document Internal and External Obstacles, Issues, Challenges, and Constraints to Achieving Program Target Goals					
	E.4- Identify and Document Categories/Classes of Opportunities					
Align the Program	A.1- Identify and Document a List of Potential Opportunities					
	A.2- Assess the Relative Risk for Each Potential Opportunity					
	A.3- Map the Potential Opportunities on a Risk-Versus-Benefit Basis					
	A.4- Prioritize the List of Opportunities					
Plan the Program	P.1- Bundle and Group Initiatives Appropriately from the Draft Strategic Agenda					
	P.2- Classify Initiatives as " Decision Focused," Change Focused," or " Quick Wins"					
	P.3- Identify Leaders for Each Initiative					
	P.4- Resource and Schedule Each Initiative					
	P.5- Establish the Leadership Team and Governance Structure/Processes					
	P.6- Align Leadership Team to Program					

Exhibit 7-11 – Checklist and assessment for completing a LEAP jump-start activity.

how five simple rules were applied across the organization. AFP operates in several commodity markets in the United States and abroad. From 1992 to 1997 the company was at the bottom-tier of its industry, with a below average total shareholder return compared to its competitors. In 1995, they began to apply these five rules in earnest.

Rule 1: Manage Value as a System

AFP addressed their strategy, assets, financial measures, and organization concurrently. The strategy that emerged was designed to move the company from its manufacturing and production focus to a marketing and customer focus. At the same time, such a strategy would be possible only if they handled their asset portfolio differently, moving from growth and acquisition to a targeted divestiture of assets. The company leaders knew that their existing portfolio was ill-suited to the new strategy. So were their financial measures. In fact, they lacked an integrated, single measure for corporate performance. So at the same time that they were reshaping strategy and shuffling assets, they adopted an economic value added (EVA) approach as the integrating financial measure of their performance. EVA was applied top to bottom, across all divisions and initiatives, and right down to the individual performers.

It was also clear that they had to concurrently remake their organization and operations. At the time, AFP was structured around asset utilization, and their executives tried to manage and use their assets as well as possible. But to pursue a customer-focused strategy, they knew they would have to become a sense-and-respond organization. From their initial determination in 1995 to apply rule one, when they were in the bottom tier in their industry, they moved by 2001 to their current position as industry leader in total shareholder return.

Rule 2: Measure the System, Not the Components

Until 1995, AFP's metrics focused primarily on manufacturing utilization. The company had seven manufacturing facilities and a variety of product lines, each of which was manufactured at a single location. With outstanding operational leaders, each of the facilities was very good at producing its products. The leaders kept utilization high and ran their plants at or near capacity. However, at most of the plants, there were far too many performance measures in place and they were often the wrong ones. Thus, judging solely by the existing manufacturing utilization measures, all of the plants were star performers.

Some of those stars faded fast when AFP, in line with its new systematic approach to value, looked at performance through the lens of corporate EVA. If the goal is to maximize EVA, then that means each facility must produce value above and beyond its cost of capital. AFP quickly discovered that some of its individual facilities were failing to meet the cost-of-capital requirement. Because the facilities had simply never been measured against EVA before, this was news—both the fact and the extent of the under-performance.

With this information in hand, the company reconsidered its entire mix of products and facilities. Once the various possibilities were analyzed, it became apparent that some of their products should not be made at all. Using their old measures, they could not have reached this conclusion. The move to a system-level, value-based measure enabled AFP to reallocate the product and manufacturing mix in line with creating maximum shareholder value.

Rule 3: Quantify Risk in Developing Strategy

Because AFP was a commodity-based company, its products eventually suffered the fate that befalls most commodities. Low-cost producers drove margins down. New competitors appeared as new technology lowered barriers to entry and turned competition into a struggle merely to maintain market share. AFP had already squeezed most of the excess costs out of its operation and was facing the downward spiral of ever-lower prices and thinner margins.

To resist the forces of commoditization, the company decided to pursue a high-margin specialty product that was sold in a spot market. The prospect of entering a new and more profitable market created great excitement. Initial evaluation of the strategy showed great promise—as much as $300 million in additional shareholder value. However, AFP had never operated in a specialty market before. Did the company have the capabilities to perform well in unfamiliar territory? Enthusiasm was tempered with caution. The new strategy entailed serious risks. The company set out to explicitly identify the sources of risk and, just as importantly, to quantify their potential impact on shareholder value.

At the top of the list of risks stood availability of products. They knew that the key to competing in a spot market is the ability to make products available quickly. The windows of opportunity are narrow and they close fast. Immediate need is what often drives customers to the spot market in the first place. Meeting that need requires an agile company; missing it means disaster. AFP determined that 60 percent of the risk associated with this strategy was tied to hitting those fleeting windows of opportunity.

The potential impact on shareholder value was enormous. If the company got availability absolutely right, it stood to increase shareholder value by as much as $700 million. Failure to master product availability could erode shareholder value by as much as half a billion dollars. The difference was enormous.

Pricing constituted the second biggest risk. Not only did they have to be able to hit the windows of opportunity at the right time, but they would have to hit them with the right price. The right timing and the right pricing were the keys to achieving the expected increase in shareholder value of $300 million and possibly as much as the entire $700 million.

After a thorough and systematic analysis of all the sources of risk, AFP concluded that fully 80 percent of the overall risk of the strategy lay in the issues of timing and pricing. The implication was clear: To minimize those risks the company would have to build a sense-and-respond organization. By explicitly identifying risk and quantifying its impact on shareholder value, AFP was able to concretely assess the upside potential as well as the downside risk and simultaneously develop a plan for managing those risks.

Rule 4: Move All Asset Portfolios onto the Efficient Frontier
In the case of Alpha Forest Products, getting on the efficient frontier included the divestiture of a business unit. As one of the

largest business-to-business organizations in a commodities market, AFP had made thirty acquisitions in the two years prior to adopting the efficient frontier approach, but it had never divested a significant asset. One of those acquisitions was a customized product company that became an AFP business unit. The unit began losing money. It was in a business that AFP had never been in before. At $250 million in annual sales in a multibillion dollar company, the unit was small, yet it required a lot of management attention.

AFP tried several times to solve the management problem, without success. The unit's performance did not improve. At best the business unit was worth about $40 million to $50 million in net present value, a pittance in the context of the corporation's NPV. The parent corporation had never considered divesting this or any other business unit, but as they began trying to move their portfolios of assets onto the efficient frontier they began to see that this small company was simply not worth much to them. So, through a targeted divestiture, AFP got well over ten times the potential operational value of the business unit.

Rule 5: Design Your Organization as a Vision of an Optimized Future State

Alpha Forest Products required large-scale changes in their organization if they were to capture the full value of their new strategy. They were moving from commodities to specialty products, from manufacturing to marketing, from multiple measures of performance to EVA as the primary measure. Each of these changes had far-reaching implications for the four major areas of organizational change:

1. *Organizational Structure:* the relation of the corporate, business units, divisions, and departments to each other and the management structures inside them and among them.

2. *The Relationship Between the Organization and Work Processes:* how the work gets done in that structure.
3. *The People:* how they are recruited, trained, retrained, incentivized, and placed in the new organization.
4. *The Culture:* how decisions are made, values are transmitted, and leadership is rewarded.

AFP had to transform itself from a slow moving, manufacturing-based organization into a sense-and-respond organization capable of anticipating the market for its products and delivering them opportunely and at the right price. Like most old-line manufacturing organizations, AFP had a hierarchical structure, with lines of command and control running vertically up and down, but rarely across, its units and departments. They moved to establish a more collegial structure, with a flatter hierarchy, so that the company could respond quickly to the market. The change in structure brought a dramatic change in the way the work got done. Instead of siloed departments and functions handing off to each other in a linear series of processes, cross-functional teams were formed in order to provide customers with complete solutions to their needs as quickly as possible.

Such a radical change required many people to unlearn old behaviors characteristic of manufacturing behemoths and learn new ones better adapted to a market where agility is all. The most dramatic change came in the culture. Decision making was decentralized. The company no longer had the luxury of being able to wait while decisions inched their way down the chain of command. Decisions had to be made close to the market, by the people who were intensely involved in customer-facing activities. Instead of lots of policies and standard operating procedures to guide day-to-day activity, the company would have to rely on the principle-based transfer of values. Employees, well versed in the company's strategy, would be expected to understand how the organization created value and act accordingly. All of this required real leadership, including leaders who could relinquish some control in return for increased shareholder value.

Make no mistake about it, significant leaps in performance require breakthrough thinking and courageous acts of leadership. The impact William Sowden Sims and Teddy Roosevelt had on improving the accuracy of naval artillery represents but one example from history of how ideas, high quality decision making, and actions came together to achieve breakthrough performance. The desire of leaders in all organizations is to achieve breakthrough performance on demand, on a repeatable and regular basis. This book presents our thinking and approaches to do just that. And this chapter presents how to gain the executive will and commitment to get jump-started.

Glossary

Change Agenda: The list of critical decisions, change projects, and continuous improvement initiatives an organization's leaders agree to pursue in the near-term (typically a six- to twelve-month window). Also known as a *strategic agenda.*

Change Leadership: The behaviors and actions the leader of an organization must demonstrate in order to effectively lead significant change in an organization (see Exhibit 2-4).

Corporate Venturing: The act of corporations participating in a broad range of potential future markets, products, and services by partnering in investment, leveraging internal assets (such as plants, processes, competencies, or intellectual property), and sharing the risk and return of these investments with the venture partners.

Cost of Capital: The expected return that is forgone by investing in a project rather than in comparable financial securities.

Decision: An allocation of resources that is revocable only at some cost.

Decision Quality: A measurement system consisting of six attributes used to qualitatively and quantitatively assess the quality of a strategic decision including: (1) appropriate frame, (2) clear value and trade-offs, (3) meaningful, reliable information, (4) creative, doable alternatives, (5) correct reasoning, and (6) commitment to action (see Chapter 2).

Divestiture: The sale, liquidation, or spin-off of a corporate division, subsidiary, or other asset.

EBITDA: Earnings before interest, taxes, depreciation, and amortization.

Economic Value Added (EVA): The difference between corporate earnings and the cost of capital resources used in a given time period such as a year.

Efficient Frontier: A curve on a graph representing the relationship between return (or another measure of benefit) and risk (or a measure of cost) for a set of investment portfolios. For a portfolio to be on the *efficient frontier*, the portfolio must maximize the return (or benefit) for a given level of risk (or cost).

Enigma: Something that is puzzling, ambiguous, or inexplicable.

Expected Productivity: A measure of expected return for a collection of investments. It is defined as the sum of the present values of the expected operating earnings (or discounted cash flows) of the investments divided by the sum of the present values of the costs to capture the earnings.

Free Cash Flow: Earnings before interest, taxes, depreciation, and amortization (EBITDA) adjusted for changes in working and fixed capital and taxes.

GAAP: Generally accepted accounting principles.

Investment Productivity Curve: A productivity curve used to measure the cumulative expected return for investments as a function of cumulative expected investment (see Chapter 3).

NPV of DCF: The net present value of discounted cash flows represents an investment's net contribution to wealth as measured in the present time period.

Pareto Rule (or Pareto Principle): The noted economist Vilfredo Pareto observed that approximately 20 percent of the peapods in his garden yielded about 80 percent of the peas that could be harvested. This concept has been abstracted to many situations as an 80/20 rule between a cause and an effect.

Portfolio Gap: The difference between the current asset portfolio and a targeted, future portfolio. The portfolio gap has two dimensions: the difference between the current *performance* of the portfolio and that of the targeted portfolio of a future state; and the difference between the current *contents* of the portfolio and the contents of the targeted portfolio in a future state.

Potential Productivity: A measure of potential return for a collection of investments defined as the sum of the present values of the potential operating earnings (or discounted cash flows) of the investments divided by the sum of the present values of the costs to capture the earnings.

Reengineering: The examination and modification of an existing system to reconstitute it in a new form and the subsequent implementation of the new form.

Risk Engineering: The extension of risk management to include the explicit consideration for maximizing the probability of a significant gain and using the identified risk to determine the problem frame and decision space.

Risk Tolerance: A measure of the extent to which an individual or corporation has an aversion to taking risks.

ROE: Return on equity, usually expressed as equity earnings as a proportion of the book value of equity.

ROI: Return on investment. Generally, book income as a proportion of net book value.

RONA: Return on net assets. Generally, book income as a proportion of net assets.

Shareholder Value: The present value of future cash flows of a business discounted by its weighted average cost of capital (WACC) less the value of debt. In simple terms, the difference between corporate value and debt.

Strategic Agenda: See Change Agenda.

Targeted Divestiture: The process by which assets are targeted for divestiture and by which possible acquirers of the assets are identified and sought.

Thought Leadership: The behaviors and actions the leader of an organization must demonstrate in order to enable the development of a creative, value-laden business strategy (see Exhibit 2-4).

Throughput: A measure of a collection of investments representing the expected fraction of the potential return of the set of investments. It is defined as the *expected productivity* divided by the *potential productivity*.

Value Based Management: A current trend in corporations typically executed as a program where economic profit is used as the primary measure of performance for activities and projects. This focuses executives and managers to take actions that will result in a measurable increase in corporate value.

Value Creation: The act of creating shareholder value.

Value Gap: The difference between the potential value of an organization or asset and its current value.

Value System: The system of four interrelated components that constitute every business organization including: (1) the business strategy, (2) the asset portfolios, (3) the financial measures and structure, and (4) the organization and operations.

Value System Diagnostic: The act of identifying and documenting the strategic actions an organization should pursue to maximize the creation of shareholder value as balanced against short-term earnings.

WACC: Weighted Average Cost of Capital. The expected return on a portfolio of all the firm's securities. It is a weighted average of the firm's cost of equity and cost of debt (see Exhibit 4-5).

Bibliography

Ackoff, Russell Lincoln, *The Democratic Corporation: A Radical Prescription for Recreating Corporate America and Rediscovering Success*. New York: Oxford University Press, 1994.

Allen, Mike, *Business Portfolio Management: Valuation, Risk Assessment, and EVA™ Strategies*. New York: John Wiley & Sons, 2000.

Amram, Martha and Nalin Kulatilaka, *Real Options: Managing Strategic Investment in an Uncertain World (Financial Management Association Survey and Synthesis Series)*. Boston: Harvard Business School Press, 1998.

Annison, Michael H., *Managing the Whirlwind: Patterns and Opportunities in a Changing World*. Englewood, N.J.: Medical Group Management Association, 1993.

Askensa, Ronald N., Ron Askensa, Lawrence A. Bossidy, Todd Jick, Steve Kerr, and Dave Ulrich, *The Boundaryless Organization: Breaking the Chains of Organization Structure, Revised and Updated*. New York: John Wiley & Sons, 2002.

Bagai, Mehrdad, Stephen Coley, and David White, *The Alchemy of Growth: Practical Insights for Building the Enduring Enterprise*. Cambridge, Mass.: Perseus Publishing, 2000.

Bartlett, Joseph W., *Fundamentals of Venture Capital*. Lanham, Md.: Madison Books, 1999.

Bazerman, Max H., *Smart Money Decisions: Why You Do What You Do with Money (and How to Change for the Better)*. New York: John Wiley & Sons, 2001.

Black, Andrew, Phillip Wright, and John Davies, *In Search of Shareholder Value: Managing the Drivers of Performance*, 2nd edition. London: *Financial Times* and Prentice Hall, 2001.

Buckingham, Marcus and Curt Coffman, *First, Break All the Rules: What the World's Greatest Managers Do*. New York: Simon & Schuster, 1999.

Christensen, Clayton M., *The Innovator's Dilemma: The Revolutionary National Bestseller That Changed the Way We Do Business*. New York: Harper Information, 2000.

Clark, Peter J. and Stephen Neill, *The Value Mandate: Maximizing Shareholder Value Across the Corporation*. New York: AMACOM, 2000.

Collins, James and Jerry I. Porras, *Built to Last: Successful Habits of Visionary Companies*. New York: Harper Collins, 1994.

Cotter, John J., *The 20% Solution: Using Rapid Redesign™ to Create Tomorrow's Organizations Today*. New York: John Wiley & Sons, 1995.

Davis, Stan M. and Christopher Meyer, *Blur: The Speed of Change in the Connected Economy*. New York: Warner Books, 1999.

Day, George S., *Market Driven Strategy: Processes for Creating Value*. New York: The Free Press, 1999.

De Geus, Arie, *The Living Company*. Boston: Harvard Business School Press, 2002.

Downes, Larry, Chunka Mui, and Nicholas Negroponte, *Unleashing the Killer App: Digital Strategies for Market Dominance*. Boston: Harvard Business School Press, 2000.

Drucker, Peter F., *Management Challenges for the 21st Century*. New York: HarperBusiness, 1999.

———*Post-Capitalist Society*. New York: HarperBusiness, 1994.

Dunlap, Albert J. and Bob Andelman (contributor), *Mean Business: How I Save Bad Companies and Make Good Companies Great*. New York: Simon & Schuster, 1997.

Ehrbar, Al, *EVA: The Real Key to Creating Wealth*. New York: John Wiley & Sons, 1998.

Evans, Philip and Thomas S. Wurster, *Blown to Bits: How the New Economics of Information Transforms Strategy*. Boston: Harvard Business School Press, 1999.

Fine, Charles H., *Clockspeed: Winning Industry Control in the Age of Temporary Advantage*. Cambridge, Mass.: Perseus, 1999.

Friedman, Thomas L., *The Lexus and the Olive Tree: Understanding Globalization*. New York: Anchor Books, 2000.

Gates, Bill and Collins Hemingway, *Business @ the Speed of Thought: Succeeding in the Digital Economy*. New York: Warner Brothers, 2000.

Gorman, Tom, Tom Richardson, and Augusto Vidaurreta, *Business Is a Contact Sport: Using the 12 Principles of Relationship Asset Management to Build Buy-in, Blast Away Barriers and Boost Your Business*. Indianapolis: Alpha Books, 2001.

Greaver, Maurice F., *Strategic Outsourcing: A Structured Approach to Outsourcing Decisions and Initiatives*. New York: AMACOM, 1999.

Hamel, Gary, *Leading the Revolution: How to Thrive in Turbulent Times by Making Innovation a Way of Life*. New York: Penguin Putnam, 2002.

Hamel, Gary and C.K. Prahalad, *Competing for the Future*. Boston: Harvard Business School Press, 1996.

Harrigan, Kathryn Rudie, *Managing Maturing Businesses: Restructuring Declining Industries and Revitalizing Troubled Operations*. Lanham, Md.: Lexington Books, 1988.

Hey, Kenneth R. and Peter D. Moore, *The Caterpillar Doesn't Know: How Personal Change Is Creating Organizational Change*. New York: The Free Press, 1998.

Hope, Jeremy and Tony Hope, *Competing in the Third Wave: The Ten Key Management Issues of the Information Age*. Boston: Harvard Business School Press, 1997.

Jonash, Ronald S. and Tom Sommerlatte, *The Innovation Premium: How Next Generation Companies Are Achieving Peak Performance and Profitability*. Cambridge, Mass.: Perseus Publishing, 2000.

Jorian, Philippe, *Value at Risk: The New Benchmark for Managing Financial Risk*. New York: McGraw-Hill, 2000.

Judson, Bruce, *Hyperwars: 11 Strategies for Survival and Profit in the Era of Online Business*. New York: Scribner, 1999.

Kanter, Rosabeth Moss, *World Class: Thriving Locally in the Global Economy*. New York: Simon & Schuster, 1997.

Kaplan, Robert S. and David P. Norton, *Balanced Scorecard: Translating Strategy into Action*. Boston: Harvard Business School Press, 1996.

————*The Strategy Focus Organization: How Balanced Scorecard Companies Thrive in the New Business Environment*. Boston: Harvard Business School Press, 2000.

Kawasaki, Guy, *How to Drive Your Competition Crazy: Creating Disruption for Fun and Profit*. Concord, Mass.: Hyperion, 1996.

Klein, Mark M. and Raymond L. Manganelli, *The Reengineering Handbook: A Step-By-Step Guide to Business Transformation*. New York: AMACOM, 1996.

Kotter, John P., *Leading Change*. Boston: Harvard Business School Press, 1996.

Labovitz, George and Victor Rosansky, *The Power of Alignment: How Great Companies Stay Centered and Accomplish Extraordinary Things*. New York: John Wiley & Sons, 1997.

Mand, Martin G. and William Whipple III, *Partnering for Performance: Unleashing the Power of Finance in the 21st-Century Organization*. New York: AMACOM, 2000.

Martin, James, *Cybercorp: The New Business Revolution*. New York: AMACOM, 1996.

Matheson, James E. and Jim Matheson, *Smart Organization: Creating Value Through Strategic R&D*. Boston: Harvard Business School Press, 1998.

McDermott, Ian and Joseph O'Connor, *The Art of Systems Thinking: Essential Skills for Creativity and Problem Solving*. New York: Thorsons Publishing, 1997.

Moore, Geoffrey A., *Living on the Fault Line: Managing for Share-*

holder Value in Any Economy. New York: HarperBusiness, 2002.

Morrison, David J. and Adrian J. Zlywotzky, *Profit Patterns: A Field Guide.* New York: Crown Publishing Group, 2000.

Ohmac, Kenichi, *The Mind of the Strategist: The Art of Japanese Business.* New York: McGraw-Hill, 1991.

Olesen, Erik, *12 Steps to Mastering the Winds of Change: Peak Performers Reveal How to Stay on Top in Times of Turmoil.* New York: Macmillan Publishing Company, 1993.

Ostroff, Frank, *The Horizontal Organization: What the Organization of the Future Actually Looks Like and How it Delivers Value to Customers.* New York: Oxford University Press, 1999.

O'Toole, James, *Leading Change: The Argument for Values-Based Leadership.* New York: Ballantine, 1996.

Pearce, Terry and David S. Pottruck, *Clicks and Mortar: Passion-Driven Growth in an Internet Driven World.* New York: John Wiley & Sons, 2001.

Pohlman, Randolph A., Gareth S. Gardiner, and Ellen M. Heffes (contributor), *Value Driven Management: How to Create and Maximize Value Over Time for Organizational Success.* New York: AMACOM, 2000.

Porter, Michael, *The Competitive Advantage: Creating and Sustaining Superior Performance.* New York: The Free Press, 1998.

———*The Competitive Strategy: Techniques for Analyzing Industries and Competitors.* New York: The Free Press, 1998.

Rodin, Robert L. and Curtis Hartman (Contributor), *Free, Perfect, and Now: Connecting to the Three Insatiable Customer Demands, A CEO's True Story.* New York: Simon & Schuster, 2000.

Rosenoer, Jonathan, Douglas Armstrong, and J. Russell Gates, *The Clickable Corporation: Successful Strategies for Capturing the Internet Advantage.* New York: The Free Press, 1999.

Schaaf, Dick, *Keeping the Edge: Giving Customers the Service They Demand.* New York: Penguin Putnam, 1997.

Schwartz, Peter, *The Art of the Long View: Paths to Strategic Insight for Yourself and Your Company*. New York: Currency Doubleday, 1996.

Senge, Peter M., Art Kleiner, Charlotte Roberts, George Roth, Rick Ross, and Bryan Smith, *The Dance of Change: The Challenges to Sustaining Momentum in Learning Organizations*. New York: Doubleday, 1999.

Simon, William L., *Beyond the Numbers: How Leading Companies Measure and Drive Success*. New York: John Wiley & Sons, 1996.

Sirower, Mark L., *The Synergy Trap: How Companies Lose the Acquisition Game*. New York: The Free Press, 1997.

Slater, Robert, *Saving Big Blue: Leadership Lessons & Turnaround Tactics of IBM's Lou Gerstner*. New York: McGraw-Hill, 2000.

Slywotzky, Adrian J., *Value Migration: How to Think Several Moves Ahead of the Competition*. Boston: Harvard Business School Press, 1996.

Smith, Douglas K., *Taking Charge of Change: 10 Principles for Managing People and Performance*. Cambridge, Mass.: Perseus Publishing, 1997.

Stack, Jack and Bo Burlington (contributor), *The Great Game of Business*. New York: Currency/Doubleday, 1994.

Stewart III, G. Bennett, *The Quest for Value: The EVA™ Management Guide*. New York: HarperBusiness, 1991.

Stross, Randall E., *Eboys: The First Inside Account of Venture Capitalists at Work*. New York: Crown Publishing Group, 2000.

Thurow, Lester C., *The Future of Capitalism: How Today's Economic Forces Shape Tomorrow's World*. New York: Penguin Putnam, 1997.

Treacy, Michael and Fred Wiersema, *Discipline of Market Leaders: Choose Your Customers, Narrow Your Focus, Dominate Your Market*. Cambridge, Mass.: Perseus Publishing, 1996.

Wasserstein, Bruce, *Big Deal: Mergers and Acquisitions in the Digital Age*. New York: Warner Books, 2001.

Wiersema, Fred, *The New Market Leaders: Who's Winning and How in the Battle for Customers.* New York: The Free Press, 2001.

Wiersema, Fred and Frederik D. Wiersema, *Customer Intimacy: Build the Customer Relationships That Ensure Your Company's Success.* New York: Warner Books, 2001.

Yoshino, Michael Y. and U. Srinivasa Rangan, *Strategic Alliances: An Entrepreneurial Approach to Globalization.* Boston: Harvard Business School Press, 1995.

Index